RESPECT *the* SPINDLE

Spin Infinite Yarns with One Amazing Tool

 Abby Franquemont

 **INTERWEAVE**
interweavestore.com

Photography, Joe Coca
Process Photography and Styling, Ann Sabin Swanson
Photo Direction + Design, Connie Poole
Production, Katherine Jackson
Technical Editor, Maggie Casey
Editor, Anne Merrow

Interweave Press LLC
201 East Fourth Street
Loveland, CO 80537-5655 USA
interweavestore.com

Printed in China by Asia Pacific Offset, Ltd.

Library of Congress Cataloging-in-Publication Data

Franquemont, Abby, 1972-
  Respect the spindle : spin infinite yarns with one
amazing tool / Abby Franquemont.
       p. cm.
  Includes bibliographical references and index.
  ISBN 978-1-59668-155-2
  1. Hand spinning. 2. Spindle-whorls. I. Title.
  TT847.F73 2009
  746.1'2--dc22
                              2009024380

10 9 8 7 6 5 4 3 2 1

acknowledgments

Thank you first and foremost to my husband and son, who've endured seemingly endless talk about this book coupled with all manner of household disaster, and still love me as much as I love them. Anne Merrow, my fearless editor, was a true partner in making this book happen quickly and beautifully. I could not ask for a finer technical editor than Maggie Casey.

So many people helped in so many ways, like all the wonderful equipment makers who loaned or donated spindles and tools. Big thanks to Tom Forrester and Jonathan Bosworth for long conversations about spindle dynamics. My dear friend Denny McMillan was a godsend both behind the scenes and for sharing the cowl she made from her first spindle-spun yarns. Thanks to Faina Letoutchaia for everything she's taught me about Russian spindles. I couldn't have pulled this off without Beth Smith and Amy King, who pitched in in too many ways to number. Thanks also to the veteran authors who cheered me on and talked me down off ledges, like Judith MacKenzie McCuin and Stephanie Pearl-McPhee.

Thank you to everyone out there who said, "You should write a book about spindles," and last but not least, to everyone at Interweave who agreed and the exceptional team who made it all happen.

To my town of Chinchero, for not letting me grow up useless; to my father, who'd have written it if he were still around; and to my mother, because really, it's all her fault (and I think we'll all agree that's a good thing).

contents

WHY THE SPINDLE?

Photo by Chris Franquemont

Since the early days of human history, spun fiber has been essential to the fabric of our lives. It fills needs so basic we can't imagine doing without them. It is the stuff of myth and legend; it is treasure beyond compare; it is commonplace and everyday. From a battered pair of favorite jeans to the carpet on our floors, and from the tents we take camping to delicate electronic components, we generally get our textiles in ready-to-use forms. They are simply there, provided for us by industry.

In the modern world, spinners have access to an incredibly broad range of tools and equipment. We can choose from every imaginable type of wheel, collect beautifully crafted spindles, and fill them with luscious fibers from all over the world—but we can also choose simple tools we make ourselves, inexpensive and improvised solutions, secondhand and salvaged equipment.

When the Spindle Rules

I learned to spin in the rural Andes of Peru. I was five years old and already alarmingly behind the curve. The elder women in town set out to remedy this by giving me a spindle—a low-whorl spindle, clunky and imperfectly balanced, weighing around 1½–2 ounces (45–60 grams). The spindle was made of a eucalyptus stick, smooth-whittled and more or less round, with a hand-carved wooden whorl. It was a typical spindle to give to a child, but adults used similar spindles for production work.

This isn't to say that some spindles weren't better than others, or that nobody had favorites; some tools seem to be better or more comfortable than others. With use and wear, many break in and get better at being tools.

So do spinners. This is a key factor in the wheel vs spindle debate. How do Andean spinners produce fine, spindle-spun high-twist yarns in quantity, using only the humblest of tools? Practice. It becomes reflexive, instinctive. That doesn't happen overnight—perhaps in years rather than weeks or months—but it does happen.

Growing Up Spinning

It took me over three years to become an adequate spinner. The year I was eight, my spinning was considered acceptable in quality by Andean standards (if slowly produced). Andean weavers require one type of yarn, fine and strong and smooth—and they are exacting judges, so this was no small feat. By this age, most girls in my peer group were spinning yarn for the family's weaving supply. Others had shown particular gifts for spinning and produced yarns for some of the town's finest weavers.

The rest of us, the merely adequate young spinners, regarded these girls with mild awe. Although it might sound like we'd spent our childhoods being sternly schooled in how to spin (and we had), our textile activities were our primary social outlet. We went out in the Inca ruins to pasture sheep, taking our spinning and weaving with us. We raced up and down hills and terraces, played tag, and gossiped. Spinning was one more game, even though we knew it was an important life skill. Those girls who were fast, perfect spinners at that age were like the girls who could sing or dance or run the fastest, only spinning was more important than that.

And we were competitive: we challenged each other to improve, constantly. By this time we were fearless with our spindles, which were never out of our hands unless we were weaving or eating. We spun while running, jumping, chasing sheep. We would pass spindles to each other while walking, talking, and spinning on them; we spun off the sides of Inca terraces, hearts pounding while the other girls watched, joking, chattering,

saying, "You can't do it! It's going to break! You'll be chasing that spindle all the way down the hill!" The really good spinners never had to chase their spindles. As for me, it was a good thing I was one of the faster kids, because I chased my spindle a lot.

With these games and challenges and the strict standards of our elders, even the completely average spinners among us became capable of production spinning. It was simply part of our lifestyle, as commonplace and essential as tying shoes or talking on the phone are in the industrialized world. My spindle was an essential part of my Andean life—of everyone's. We were never without our spindles.

Enter the Wheel

Later that same year, back in the United States, I encountered my first spinning wheels. One was an antique Shaker-made great wheel my parents had found. This was the first wheel I learned to use and also the first type of wheel widely adopted by spinners who had spent thousands of years using spindles. Great wheels are the oldest and simplest of the lot: a large wheel that drives a horizontal spindle.

That summer, when my parents were demonstrating Andean weaving at a nearby craft fair, I encountered another type of spinning wheel: the treadle-driven bobbin-and-flyer wheel. Unlike the great wheel, these require the spinner to be seated, working the treadles to make a drive wheel turn.

Having finally been deemed a near-adequate spinner by Andean standards, I scorned the flyer wheels; they were interesting, but seemed almost gimmicky. What's more, the spinners I saw using these wheels were producing thick, floppy, often uneven yarn that

Spindle-spun singles from a wool/silk/camel blend.

Chinchero girls are constantly socializing over spinning and weaving work.

my Andean teachers would never have accepted as functional.

By the time I was ten, I had learned to spin long-draw woolen yarns with the great wheel. But there were two problems. First, because of the great wheel's size, I couldn't take it anywhere with me; I had to use it at home, in the room where it lived. Second, I couldn't use those soft woolen yarns for Andean weaving, my fiber art of choice. Ultimately, I turned back to my spindle, which could go anywhere with me and produce the yarns I wanted to use.

Reconsidering the Wheel

It wasn't until my late twenties that I decided I wanted to spin for crochet and knitting. I had received freshly shorn alpaca from someone who raised the animals, and I wanted to make her a scarf from her own animals' fiber. I

wanted a lofty, fuzzy yarn without a lot of twist in it, and because I wanted to finish it in time for her birthday, I would also need thicker yarn than I usually spun. I picked up one of my simple spindles and set to work.

My first several results were not at all what I wanted. They were thicker, but they were dense, not lofty. Reluctantly, I concluded that I might want a spinning wheel to achieve my goal, and I ended up with one of the very wheels I'd scorned years before. I was spinning yarn the Andean teachers of my childhood would never have accepted, but that was perfect for knitting and crocheting. With practice and some good advice, I was able to produce it in large quantities very quickly.

I decided to see how much faster I could produce Andean-style weaving yarn with my new tool. What an

exercise in futility and boredom! I simply couldn't do it fast enough—yet it was a trifle to do with a spindle. I still spin Andean weaving yarn faster with a low-whorl spindle than anything else. That simplest of tools is truly the best one for that job. I found that wheels and spindles—and even different types of spindles—were a range of equipment with specialties, and that no single one could perfectly fulfill every spinning desire I might have. I would need different tools to do different things.

Community of Spindle Spinners

Talking with other spinners, I would sometimes find that they were shocked I'd choose the spindle over the wheel for some things. "Isn't that slower?" one friend asked. "It really isn't," I told her. "I can spin on the go, or in small spaces, or in short bursts here and there. But another factor is what kind of yarn you're spinning, from what kind of fiber. You should try it for gossamer lace yarns. I think you'll see it's faster than you think." For some of my friends, the spindle really was just as fast; for others, it simply was not. I came to realize that many modern spinners didn't know the spindle techniques I had taken for granted since childhood.

I also came to know spindle spinners from other cultures: cotton spinners from Africa and Central America, Orenburg lace knitters from Russia, so many spindle spinners with different spindle traditions and techniques that made it possible for them to do things they couldn't reproduce with a wheel. I met spinners who had wheels, but rarely used them, or only used them for specific tasks. I met spinners who didn't have the means to afford expensive equipment and large quantities of fiber, who wanted to get the most bang for the buck out of making their own yarn.

I met enthusiastic spinners who wanted to like spindles, but didn't—and often when we sat and talked, it would come out that they had simply never had a chance to learn more than the very basics of using a spindle, or they had been told it could only be slower than a wheel, or was just a low-cost way of deciding whether they liked spinning enough to buy a wheel.

Production Spindle Spinning

Using a spindle to produce major quantities of yarn requires more of the spinner than producing the same volume with a wheel. There is a longer learning curve. Once you commit to it and achieve the comfort level required to use the tool in a production capacity, you can do tremendous things with it, even outperform more technologically advanced tools. That's true for most technologies, and textile production is no exception.

Producing textile goods has been a driving force behind vast amounts of technological development and changes in lifestyle. The need to produce textiles is very real, and it's necessary to do it with speed and efficiency. In the Andean

town where I spent so much of my childhood, tremendous levels of productivity were achieved due to childhood training and the number of people involved. In the industrialized world, the need to produce textiles is solved more by mechanization than by lifelong training, which could be said about many things in modern life.

The spindle is a simple tool. It is a hammer, a straight saw, a chisel, a source of heat, a pot or pan, a knife, a pen. Where the spinning wheel is a printing press, a spindle is a pen. Both require skill and training to operate, and there are things you can do with one that you can't do with the other. The spinning wheel is one of the core machines upon which civilization is built.

Mechanization isn't bad—it is a natural solution to many problems—but it has its down sides. Once a machine is developed to perform a task, people start to lose the skill to do that task without the machine. That's part of why I think we now believe, and accept so readily, that wheels are just faster. It's true that they are, for some things. But not for all. Most of us never have the chance to develop the skills that made spindles so ubiquitous a tool for most of human history. We tend to move on quickly to things that get us results faster, without exploring the results we never knew were possible with the simpler tool.

I urge spinners not to simply skip the spindle altogether or view it as only a low-cost starter tool that will help you

to decide if you want to do this enough to spend the money on a wheel. Spinning on a wheel and spinning on a spindle are the same, and not. They are related, and they're totally different.

Spin Every Day

I never leave the house without a spindle and some fiber in my bag. Spinning on the go, a skill I learned in early childhood, is easy for me. I can do it while I'm doing almost anything else. It's more portable, more forgiving, than many knitting or crochet projects, and it is simply part of my way of life.

My evolution as a spinner is still in progress. That's one of the reasons I love to spin: no matter how long I live and how many things I learn about spinning, there will always be more to explore, more to try, and more to achieve. There are always many ways to do it, and many perspectives—and those perspectives can shift. But one thing I'm sure of is this: No matter how I change, I'll never give up my spindles. I'm grateful for the deep, almost spiritual connection with fiber that they allow me and for the range of options they provide.

For me and many other spindle spinners, nothing compares to the freedom, portability, and simple elegance of these ancient tools and what they can do in skilled hands. This book is an homage to spindles and an opportunity to share the joy and accomplishment that spinners have found working with them for thousands of years.

Know about Spindles

There are many kinds of spindles and many ways to use them.

There is far more to be said on the subject than could ever fit

in just one book, but this overview will get you started choosing

and working with a wide variety of these wonderful tools.

CHOOSING a SPINDLE

It can be hard to know what spindle is the right one for you. Spinners have personal preferences, and you will probably spin on a variety of spindles before you settle on favorites. There is no simple answer to the question of what is the best spindle for starting out, but there are some common factors that can help you discover where your own preferences lie.

If you have the opportunity to visit a shop that carries spinning supplies, you will likely find people who will be delighted to help you choose what you need to get started spinning. If you're mail-ordering supplies, advice may be harder to find. Either way, this chapter should help put you on the road to spindle success.

Types of Spindles

In the family of spindles, there are two types of spindles, and within those, many subcategories; these distinctions are largely based on how they are used. The first type is the suspended spindle (or drop spindle), so called because it spins hanging from the yarn it is being used to produce. The spinner sets it in motion and drops it, leaving it to spin. The second type is the supported spindle, which doesn't hang suspended from the yarn it is forming; there is always something bearing at least part of its weight.

With a suspended spindle, the yarn must already be sufficiently formed to bear the weight of the spindle before that weight is introduced to it. With a supported spindle, the yarn being formed does not have to be load-bearing, and this enables you to spin using a different range of techniques than would be possible if the yarn had to hold the weight of the spindle as you go.

Suspended or Drop Spindles

There are a few major species of suspended spindles, mostly differentiated by where the whorl is placed on the shaft. The weight of high-whorl spindles is placed at or near the top of the shaft; on low whorls it is at or near the bottom. There are also some spindles where a whorl is placed at the middle of the shaft, which have historically been used both as suspended and supported spindles.

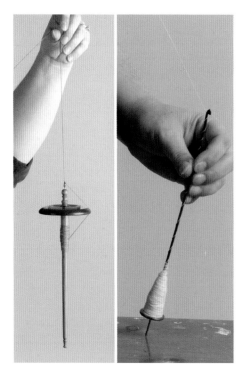

Left: Spinning suspended.
Right: Spinning supported.

Each of these spindle species includes a wide variety of breeds—there is as much difference between top whorls as there is between dogs. There are tiny lap dogs, big husky working dogs, and everything in between. The same is true for every species of spindle; there is a seemingly endless range of choices.

anatomy of the low-whorl spindle

The simplest low-whorl spindle consists of a shaft and a weight placed at or near the shaft's bottom. The shaft may have a hook or a notch near the top to make it easier to secure spun yarn to the spindle. If the spindle does not have a hook or a notch, a half-hitch is typically used to secure yarn (see page 56).

The whorl is generally not at the exact bottom of a low-whorl spindle; there is usually a little bit of the shaft protruding, often pointed. The cop, or already-spun yarn stored on the spindle shaft, is usually wound close to the whorl, but it doesn't have to be—you could wind it anywhere.

Low-whorl spindles are common all over the world and used for almost all types of fiber.

anatomy of the high-whorl spindle

A high-whorl (sometimes called top-whorl) spindle bears its weight at or near the top of the shaft. Nearly all high-whorl spindles have a hook for securing your spun yarn to the spindle.

Some high whorls have one or more notches in the whorl to help keep yarn from slipping around the whorl and the hook and coming off the spindle unbidden.

In most high-whorl spindles, the whorl is so close to the top of the shaft that there would be no way to secure your spun yarn with a half-hitch (see page 56). When you wind yarn onto a high-whorl spindle, you wind it below the whorl, usually as close to the whorl as you can.

High-whorl spindles have historically been found in Scandinavian countries and have a longer history of spinning long-stapled or mixed-length fibers than short, downy fibers; however, those found in Africa were clearly used with cotton.

anatomy of a mid-whorl spindle

A mid-whorl spindle has its weight in the middle of the shaft. Some feature a hook or a notch at one end and a point at the other. The cop on a mid-whorl spindle is typically wound between the whorl and the hook or notch.

Mid-whorl spindles are most common in Southeast Asia, though African spindles with beads for whorls often have the bead placed closer to the middle than the bottom.

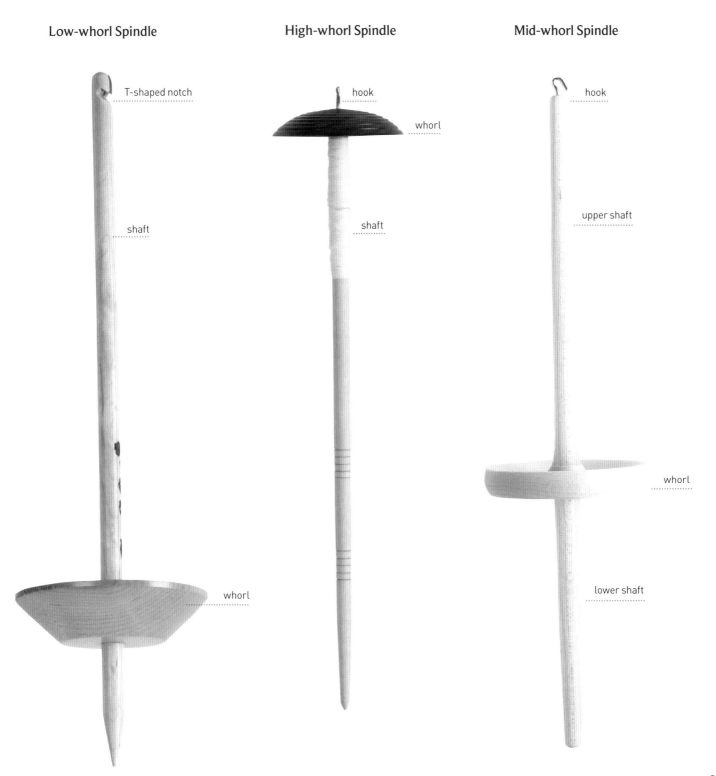

Low-whorl Spindle

T-shaped notch

shaft

whorl

High-whorl Spindle

hook

whorl

shaft

Mid-whorl Spindle

hook

upper shaft

whorl

lower shaft

Supported Spindles

Supported spindles come in two main species. The first operate like suspended spindles, except that they touch the ground, a bowl, or another surface (such as the tahkli at right). Once these spindles are set in motion, you let go of the spindle and let its bottom rest on its support while you get on with drafting, either with one or two hands.

The second type of supported spindles still don't hang suspended, but instead of always resting on a surface, you may hold one in your hand twirling or constantly support it with your hand as well as another surface (such as the French spindle at right). When you spin with these spindles, one hand is constantly touching (or almost touching) the spindle, and you will only have one hand available to draft.

Some supported spindles are simply shafts with no separate whorl, where the shaft is shaped to be comfortable to the hand and easy to twirl. These are intended to be used while held in hand. Others are intended to rest on a surface, and these tend to have sharply pointed bottoms to reduce friction from that surface when in use.

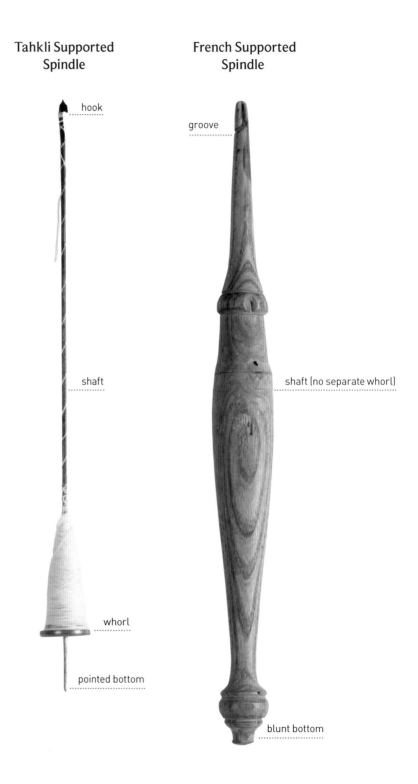

Tahkli Supported
Spindle

hook

shaft

whorl

pointed bottom

French Supported
Spindle

groove

shaft (no separate whorl)

blunt bottom

Hooks, Notches, and Hitches

For suspended spinning, it is absolutely necessary to secure the yarn you've already spun and wound onto your spindle so that it won't just all come off when you start to spin. If it does, you can't spin a new length of yarn, and the yarn you have already spun and stored is at risk of being damaged or lost.

A hook is placed on a spindle so that the yarn coming through it will emerge as close as possible to the axis of rotation. They can be found on high-whorl, mid-whorl, and low-whorl drop spindles, and sometimes on support spindles as well.

Low-whorl spindles may allow you to secure your yarn in a variety of ways: Some have hooks to secure your yarn, while others have notches on the shaft. Others feature shaping at the shaft's end, and still others have smooth shafts with no hook, notch, or shaping to speak of. Some have hooks that can be easily removed. You might find it a challenge to secure your yarn with half-hitches (see page 56), or you might find it uncomfortable to spin with the wrong hook or with yarn that isn't directly centered over the shaft.

Low-whorl Shafts

no hook   flared   hook

Hook Varieties

tall squared hook   low-profile hook   tall slim hook   cup hook

Notch Varieties

Supported Spindle Varieties

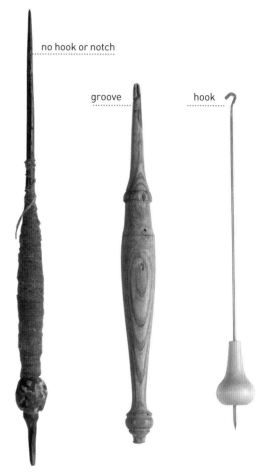

notches all
around whorl

single notch
behind hook

three notches
around whorl

no hook or notch

groove

hook

Notches of various kinds can also be found on any variety of spindle. Some are intended to prevent yarn from slipping off the shaft, while others are carefully constructed to work like hooks do, bringing the yarn as close as possible to the central axis of rotation. Some spindles feature a hook or notch in the shaft or atop the whorl, paired with a notch in the whorl.

These are intended to keep yarn from slipping once wound on and secured with the hook. They vary in the size and shape of the hook, whether there is a notch in the whorl, and where the notch is placed. As you develop your personal spinning style, you will probably prefer one type of hook and notch placement over another, but they all work well. For many new spinners, a notch placed exactly behind the hook is easiest to manage. Some supported spindles feature hooks or notches at the tip to prevent spun yarn from sliding off as you spin; others do not.

Most of the oldest spindles we know about don't have hooks or notches at all. Instead, they may have a little bit of shaping at the tip. If there is shaping that bulges outward, it's usually intended to keep yarn secured with a half-hitch from slipping off. If there is shaping that tapers to a point, it's generally so that you can spin off the point or so that you can start the spindle in motion easily by flicking and get higher speeds from that flick. (Sometimes spindles that started with no shaping become tapered simply from being used.)

Selecting a Spindle

Whether you're choosing your first spindle or your twentieth, there are several questions to ask before deciding which is right for you. The first question is simple: What do you like to spin? Is there a type of yarn that you like to work with? A specific fiber you intend to spin? Or are you just looking for a general jumping-off point?

If you're interested in making a specific yarn, check out Which Spindle When on page 90, which discusses many specialty spindles and the yarns and fibers to which they are suited. Even a complete novice can go straight to specialty spindles. There is no absolute path to spindle mastery throughout history and around the world; you don't have to follow one single path either.

To find that general starting point, though, let's assume you can choose any spindle you desire and any fiber you can name. As you look for your first spindle, here are some questions you should ask yourself.

Contemporary spinners typically focus on suspended spindles, and that's where we're starting out. If you prefer to start supported, there's no reason you can't.

Low Whorl or High Whorl?

There is a lot of conventional wisdom about which type of spindle is better or easier to spin with, but this will come down to your personal preference. If you're new to this, you don't have a personal preference yet, so how do you decide?

You don't have to! Just get one of each. Even if you feel drawn to one over the other, you should try each one, and what you find might surprise you. Many spinners who assumed they would prefer a high whorl have been shocked to discover they actually are more comfortable with a low-whorl spindle, and vice versa.

In general, low-whorl spindles are more stable and harder to unbalance. This has made them a popular choice for beginning spinners for many years, and it's a key reason why low-whorl spindles

Buying Your First Spindle

* Choose both a low-whorl and a high-whorl spindle if you can.
* Look for spindles weighing 1–2 ounces (30–60 grams).
* Don't worry too much about the hook or notch configuration; as your skills develop you may form a preference.
* Look for simple, durable materials.

MAKING A TOY WHEEL SPINDLE

If you'd rather make an inexpensive spindle than buy your first, it's easy to make a functional spindle with a toy wheel and dowel, supplies from a local craft or home-supply store.

Toy wooden wheels come with holes pre-drilled in them, and dowels can easily be found in the same sizes. Make sure these match up; if your toy wheel has a ¼" hole, you will need a ¼" dowel 8"–12" long to make a spindle.

Simply put the toy wheel on the dowel. It will likely be a snug fit, and you may need to pound to get the dowel all the way through. That's fine; you want it to fit tightly enough that the wheel does not slip off.

Place the wheel about 1" from the end of the shaft. If you would like to use this spindle with a low whorl, you're all set! You may wish to sand the spindle lightly to remove any rough spots that could catch your fingers or your yarn. If you'd like to use it as a high whorl, gently screw a cup hook into the end near the whorl.

If you would like the spindle to be a bit heavier, slip one or more washers onto the shaft above the whorl.

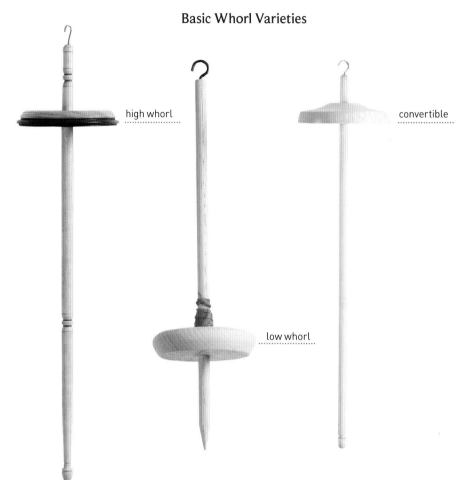

Basic Whorl Varieties

high whorl

low whorl

convertible

have prevailed around the world through much of history. It's simply easier to make a dependable, well-performing low-whorl spindle than a high-whorl spindle. A low-whorl spindle is more tolerant of minor flaws—a slightly bent shaft, shaft out of round, whorl a little off balance—than a high-whorl spindle.

In the modern world, master spindle-crafters can create anything they choose with great precision. Longstanding obstacles in making a great high-whorl spindle are essentially erased by technical accuracy. High whorls have become a more popular choice than low whorls (or the lesser-known mid-whorls) in many areas, and you may find more beautiful and well-made high-whorl spindles on the market than any other type.

Another option is the convertible spindle, which can be used as either a low whorl or a high whorl. Some spindles are specifically designed to be used either way, but in some cases it's just a happy accident. You may be able to flip a high whorl over and use it as a low whorl in a pinch, but it's usually harder to do that with a low whorl. Low whorls may not be as precisely balanced as high whorls, and most high whorls require a hook to secure your yarn as you spin.

What Is a Good Weight?

The weight of a spindle can be a huge factor in a new spinner's success and enjoyment, although it is also subject to personal preferences that develop over time. By and large, very light spindles are well suited to spinning very fine yarn, and very heavy spindles tend to do better with thicker yarn. If your spindle is too light for the yarn you're trying to spin, it will stop moving and you'll have no luck; if it's too heavy, your

yarn may break or drift apart as it is forming. Either of these scenarios can be extremely frustrating and a huge obstacle to overcome.

Most contemporary spinners succeed fastest using spindles weighing 1 to 2 ounces (30 to 60 grams). Spindles lighter than an ounce often lack the momentum to keep putting twist into a new spinner's yarn and thus won't spin long enough for you to get your fiber drafted and yarn spun. New spinners often find light

Various Whorl Materials

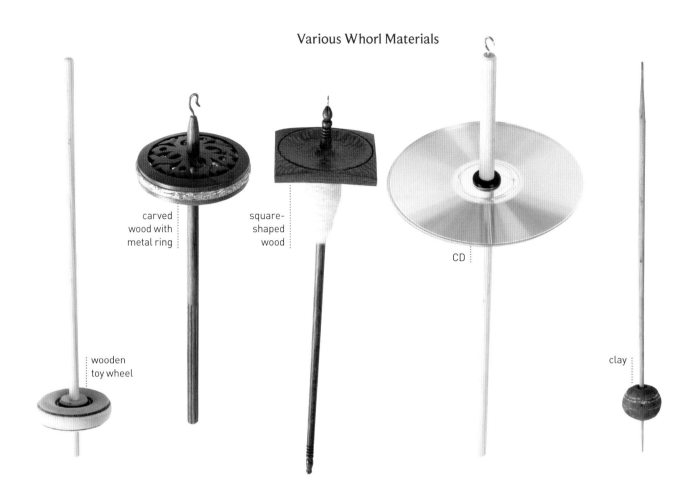

carved
wood with
metal ring

square-
shaped
wood

CD

wooden
toy wheel

clay

spindles prone to backspinning—they may stop spinning in the direction you started them in and spin the other way instead. Spindles weighing over 2 ounces may break the delicate yarn as it is form-ing or continue spinning for so long that you end up with far more twist than you or your yarn can handle.

What Kind of Material?

Spindles are made from many things! Spindle shafts are most commonly wooden, though some are metal. Whorls can be made from wood, ceramic, polymer clay, glass beads, plastic, or practically anything at all. There are beautiful spindle whorls made from beads and carved stones. On some the whorl and shaft are all one piece and others are multiple joined pieces. Not all whorls are round. They don't have to be—they just need to be balanced enough that your spindle rotates comfortably. Compact discs and toy wheels are popular choices for whorls on inexpensive spindles you can make yourself (see page 19).

You may not want to start out with anything too ornate or fragile because there is every chance your spindle will suffer a few sudden falls as you learn. The most durable are simple wooden or solid ceramic whorls; some of the oldest whorls found as artifacts are ceramic and date back thousands of years. Both of these materials can still be broken, but they usually do hold up well.

THE SCIENCE OF SPINDLES

There is no way to be certain exactly how old the handspindle is as a tool. We do know it is very ancient, older than civilization as we know it, and has existed in many thousands of forms. Despite its simplicity as a tool, understanding all the scientific angles is extremely complicated, and relatively little study has been done from a physics or engineering perspective. A spindle's secrets can be hard to unlock without the techniques that go with them, and from an archaeological perspective, many ancient spindles remain mysterious as well. In this chapter, we'll give a rough overview to get you started thinking about the science of spindles.

The more kinds of spindles—and spindle techniques—you know about, the more you may be able to tell simply from trying to use the tool. As a spinner, you know what you're trying to accomplish, and just setting out to do so can be incredibly informative. Yet the simpler the tool, the more options exist for its use. As with so many things about spinning, there is really no one true way it's done, and it's impossible to define rigid absolutes. That's not our goal—we just want you to have an overview of the ideas to help you think through spindle behaviors you may already know and understand. Simply put, we're going for "Why does it do that?" instead of exact formulae.

On the Origin of Spindles

Sometimes I like to imagine a world before spun yarn, a world in which there were no textiles. It's easy (if not pleasant) to picture what life might be like with no clothing, but what about all the other things made from yarn, or the skills and technology that go along with making yarn? Simply obtaining food and shelter would be very hard with no fishing lines, game nets, or animal tethers. There would have been no thatch lashed to branches to put roofs over our heads. We needed to attach stone axe-heads to shafts and make ropes for pulleys and simple machines; we needed baskets and net bags to carry our stuff. Sinews and found fibers only get us so far. There

This Guatemalan supported spindle was developed to spin short-staple cotton.

is a very real, universal human need for yarn, rope, and cordage going back thousands and thousands of years in most of the cultures of the world.

You can see on page 53 how a simple stick makes producing and storing yarn feasible. I envision our enterprising prehistoric ancestors making sticks or perhaps bones into specialized yarn-producing tools. I figure some said, "If I put a weight on this stick in the first place, it would go around faster to begin with, and I could make yarn fast all

the time." Others thought, "You know, I could carve this stick in different shapes and make it easier to twirl." From such beginnings, handspindles evolved all over the world, ultimately being developed and refined over many generations into the perfect hand tool for spinning yarn from the fibers that were available.

Although it's hard to make definitive generalizations about the history of the ancient tool, evidence suggests supported spindles and the techniques that go with them evolved predominantly

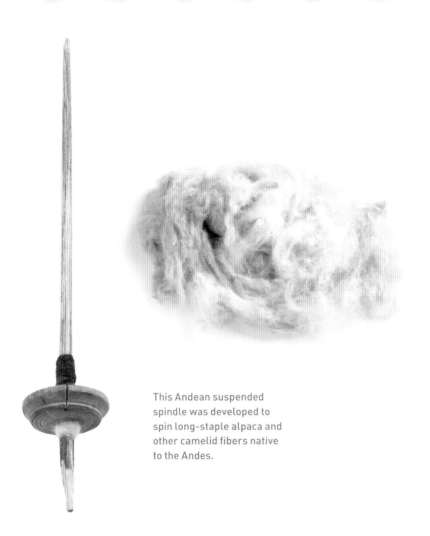

This Andean suspended spindle was developed to spin long-staple alpaca and other camelid fibers native to the Andes.

overview, there is likely to still be a small-brush detail that's an exception. I hope that this chapter will serve you well in considering your own spinning options—and launch further research of your own, if you are so inclined.

Modes of Use

We'll discuss two major ways of using spindles: suspended (or hanging from the yarn you're spinning) and supported (where the yarn being spun does not bear the weight of the spindle directly). There are variations on these themes, including methods for spinning both supported and suspended while producing yarn, but understanding these two main modes of use is a good starting point for taking your spindle spinning in any direction you choose.

Most spindles have two main features: a shaft and a whorl that serves as a weight. However, spindles do not always feature a distinct whorl; many spindles intended for supported use are made from one solid piece of wood shaped either to be twirled in the hand or spun while resting in a bowl or on a surface. Most spindles designed for suspended use could potentially be used supported, but the opposite is not always true—many support spindles would absolutely not work well as drop spindles.

where the available materials are short-stapled. African countries have always been strong producers of cotton, and much pan-Asian livestock produce short-stapled downy fibers; supported spindles have long been common in both areas. By contrast, areas where the available fiber was largely longer-stapled (such as sheep's wool or flax) have tended to develop suspended spindles, although this isn't universally the case.

We may never know everything we'd like to about the origins of spindles.

Indeed, some researchers believe they may have been in use even before language. The origin of spindles is a subject still in dire need of research and investigation. Because of the spindle's simplicity, evaluating how spindles in archaeological finds were used calls for expert spinners to help think it through, but not all archaeologists are spinners. With so lengthy and widespread a history, it's difficult to generalize; anywhere we paint with broad strokes to give a general

The Physics of Spindles

Regardless of where the whorl is placed, the weight of a suspended spindle is at the bottom of your yarn, making it behave like a pendulum—a weight suspended on a cord. But the shape of that weight and how it's distributed make spindles like tops, which keep spinning once set in motion. A drop spindle is like a top on the end of a string.

Like a spindle, a top rotates around a central axis, continuing to spin until external forces cause it to slow and eventually stop. That central axis, right in the middle of all the spinning action, is where the top's center of gravity needs to be to keep it spinning as long as possible. On a spindle, this is where the shaft is.

In theory, if a top were spun in a vacuum and without touching anything, there would be nothing to stop it from turning except for slight variations in mass distribution, which would eventually cause the top to wobble (or precess). Once it starts to wobble, it isn't rotating exactly around its original axis of rotation; as it slows to a near stop it will wobble more and more until ultimately it falls over and stops. In practice, a top in motion is also affected by friction from the air and on its base where it touches the ground, as well as other possible forces like wind or human interference.

Drop spindles need to be able to rotate around a central axis, but unlike tops, they hang suspended from something (the yarn you are spinning), and gravity is constantly working to bring them back to alignment with the axis of rotation. When a top spins, the twist energy it generates is dissipated into thin air. When a spindle spins, that twist energy goes into the yarn. Even as gravity tries to pull the spindle back to its central axis whenever it wobbles, the yarn is also storing twist energy that will act against the spindle's rotation.

Where a spindle used in suspended-spinning mode is more like a pendulum than a top, spindles used in supported-spinning mode are more like a top than a pendulum.

The elements in play with all spindles, whether used supported, suspended, or otherwise, are:

* Mass
* Shape
* Mass distribution
* Balance
* Friction
* Yarn being spun
* Human interaction and other factors

The first four are physical attributes of the spindle itself; the last three are more variable and unpredictable. Each is important to how your spindle will behave and how it will work for you personally. How each of these factors affects your experience with a given spindle is unavoidably subjective, but understanding the principles is helpful

Spindles and tops both rotate around a central axis, but the energy of the spindle's rotation goes into the spun yarn instead of the air.

in evaluating a spindle you're trying out. You can't discount your body mechanics, the setting in which you wish to spin, what fibers you're spinning, and what kind of yarn you're planning. Spindles do not spin in a vacuum, which makes it impossible to choose one single shape, weight, or size, and call it ideal.

Mass

The heavier an object is (with more distributed mass, in scientific terms), the more force is required to get it started moving or make it stop moving. This effect is in direct proportion to the mass of the object. In layman's terms, if you have a spindle that weighs 10 grams, it requires a 10-gram flick to get it going; a spindle that weighs 40 grams needs a 40-gram flick. The flip side is that to slow it down and stop it, your 10-gram spindle requires 10 grams worth of counteracting forces (like gravity, wind resistance, human interaction, or twist energy from the yarn) to bring it back to a standstill. The heavier 40-gram spindle, though, needs 40 grams worth of those same counteracting forces.

In other words, a heavier spindle can withstand more forces acting against its rotation than a lighter spindle. A spindle with greater mass will always have greater momentum, or tendency to stay in motion, than a similarly shaped spindle with less distributed mass.

The heavier spindle at left requires more force to start and stop than the lighter one on the right.

Shape

How an object is shaped has several effects, not least on mass distribution and balance. It affects how you can hold the spindle, how you can use it, and how outside forces act on it. Some shapes depend on having other forces act on them in certain ways while the object is in motion. For example, a spindle meant to be used supported may not work well as a suspended spindle because its shape may require constant input to keep it in motion. The shape of a spindle may limit where you can place your cop or grasp it to set it in motion. This is as true for spindles as for tops.

Mass Distribution

Top-heavy items are more prone to tipping over than things that are bottom heavy. You may have noticed that if you're trying to tip something over that's standing on the ground, it takes less force to tip it by pushing at the top than in the middle or the bottom. When you're making things that stand on the ground and you want them to resist tipping over, you put the heaviest and widest part as close to the ground as possible. This is because gravity will always pull straight down. An object standing on the ground won't tip over as long as the center of mass (where the weight is concentrated) is over the part that touches the ground when gravity pulls straight down. As soon as the center of mass moves farther out so it isn't over the base

Spindles don't have to have round whorls! Balance doesn't depend on being perfectly round, but rather on even distribution around the center of rotation. Many delightful spindles come in a wide range of shapes.

of the object anymore, it will tip over. Something with a wide, flat base is more stable on the ground than something with a small, narrow base.

The rules change with an object that doesn't touch the ground, but the importance of mass distribution doesn't go away. Ancient Greek scientist Archimedes tested this, and so can you: if you float a tube with a heavy end and a light end in a basin of water, the heavy end will always end up on the bottom. If the heavy part is in the middle, then the tube will lie on its side as it floats.

Suspended spindles neither float in water (at least, I can't think of a good reason for them to) nor touch the ground. Instead, they hang from a string, and the rules change again—neither a ground-standing object nor a floating object behaves the same as an object suspended in mid-air. Adding a string seems like a simple change, but we're now discussing a device physicists call a *torsion pendulum*: a weight suspended from a wire, able to rotate around a central axis.

On one hand, it seems obvious that the central axis—the axis of rotation—would be the spindle's shaft. But this isn't the whole story. The axis of rotation is affected by the string from which the object hangs, and the spindle sways like a pendulum from side to side and possibly around in a circle. Going back to how center of mass affects stability, if the center of mass is as close as possible

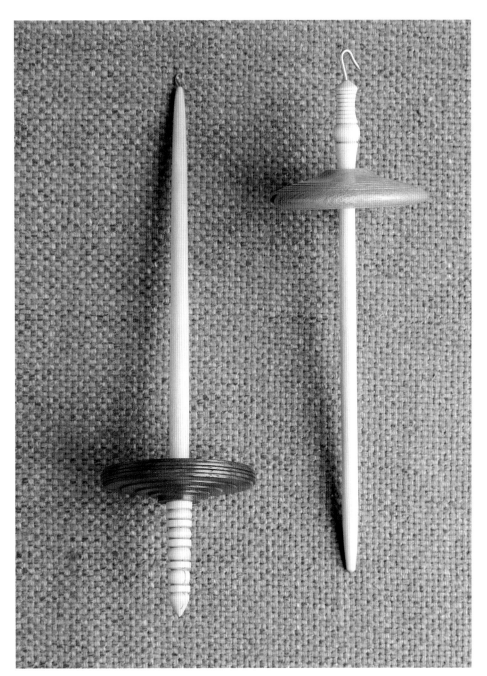

A spindle with a weight at or near the bottom (a low-whorl spindle) is more stable and resistant to disruption by external forces than one with weight at or near the top (a high-whorl spindle).

to the end of the pendulum, the center of mass is close to the ground; if it is farther from the end of the pendulum, it's higher up.

top-heavy vs bottom-heavy

A spindle with the mass toward the bottom is less prone to tipping over (and thus losing energy to wobble, causing a more rapid slowdown) than one that is weighted higher up. In practical terms, a spindle with the center of mass located near the bottom (a low-whorl spindle) is more stable and more resistant to being disrupted by external forces. A spindle with the center of mass located higher up (a high-whorl spindle) is more vulnerable to upset and more likely to slow down or stop if it is wobbly.

If you are making a spindle with the center of mass located higher up the shaft, you have to do everything possible to make sure it is not prone to any sort of wobbling. A spindle with the center of mass located near the bottom is likelier to keep spinning even when it wobbles, which all spindles do to at least some degree.

Though closely related to mass distribution (which relates to where the center of mass is placed vertically along the spindle's shaft), overall spindle balance also involves how mass is distributed horizontally, radiating out or away from the spindle's shaft and the axis of rotation.

Mass Distribution and Rotational Dynamics

If the center of mass is close to the axis of rotation, then your object can spin significantly faster than if the center of mass is more spread out or is concentrated away from the axis of rotation. The classic example is a figure skater who starts rotating with arms outstretched, then pulls them in, speeding up tremendously. If the skater extends her arms again, she slows down. She is redistributing her mass.

There are several factors in play here. The first is what physicists call the moment of inertia (or MI), which is a measurement of how hard it is to change the way a spinning object moves around its axis of rotation. It's similar to the concept of momentum—how an object in motion will tend to stay in motion. The major difference is that now we're talking about a specific motion: rotating.

When something solid rotates, the whole object rotates at a constant rate. If the center turns 5 times per minute, so does the outside. However, the distance around the outside is much greater than the distance around the center; the outside has to go farther in the same amount of time, so it goes faster in order to turn the same number of times per minute. Place a mark near the center of a disc rotating 5 times per second—say, at the point where the circumference of the disc is 10 cm. That point is traveling at 50 cm per minute. But if we place a mark farther out from the center, where

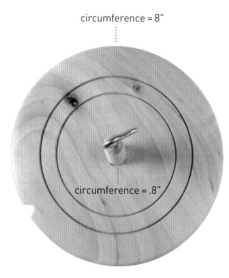

Each time a point on the inner circumference travels .8", a corresponding point on the outer circumference travels 8", or 10 times faster.

the circumference is 20 cm, that mark is moving twice as fast as the point in the center, or 100 cm per second.

This means that the outside of that disc needs more force (called torque) to keep pushing it through the air because it has to go faster to turn the same number of times per minute. So if the disc is wider—with a larger radius—it will be harder to get started and harder to stop than one with a smaller radius. So it's reasonably accurate to say that a spindle with a wider whorl will tend to keep rotating more than one with a narrower whorl. It has a higher moment of inertia than a narrower-whorled spindle would have.

There's more to the picture, however. Going back to the figure skater, her highest moment of inertia occurs while she has her arms outstretched. She is rotating and has the force to keep rotating—and then she pulls her

A spindle with mass concentrated close to the shaft tends to spin faster, while a spindle with mass placed far from the shaft tends to spin longer.

arms in. She immediately starts to spin faster, because that same amount of force is still in play, and now less of it is needed to keep pushing the outside around. Physicists and engineers call this principle the conservation of angular momentum. Because the amount of energy required to make her turn when her arms are stretched out doesn't change, and because that energy doesn't go away just because she pulls in her arms, she speeds up.

This principle doesn't apply cleanly to spindles because a spindle can't just pull in its arms and speed up, but you can see the premise in action when you compare spindles.

rim-weighted vs center-weighted

A spindle with a large, heavy whorl that concentrates mass closer to the axis of

rotation—the shaft—will spin faster than one with a large, heavy whorl that concentrates its mass toward the outside. The center-loaded spindle is like a figure skater with her arms pulled in close; the rim-loaded spindle is like a skater with her arms outstretched. Looking again at the moment of inertia, we see that the center-loaded spindle will be easier to start and stop, and the rim-loaded

spindle will be harder.

Shaft diameter is another way spindles provide different kinds of mechanical advantage. A narrower shaft makes it easier to set the spindle in motion more quickly than a thicker one but may be a little harder to set in motion. A thicker shaft may be easier to get started but will result in a slower spin.

Friction

Whenever we move around, we are touching other things and moving against them. Even the air around us has substance, and simply moving through the air requires energy. (Remember that next time you're having a slow-starting morning.) When objects move against each other, the force that's generated by that action is called friction. It's sort of a grinding, dragging action. Supported spindles often have sharply pointed bottoms and are used with special bowls to reduce friction. You don't notice friction from the air when you wave your hand around at

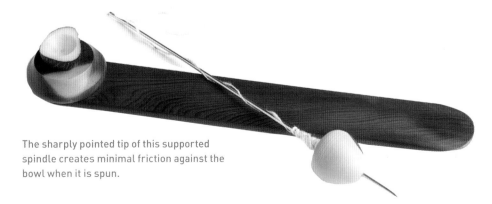

The sharply pointed tip of this supported spindle creates minimal friction against the bowl when it is spun.

Winding a cop on a spindle increases its mass and changes how the mass is distributed.

normal speeds, but if you were that figure skater with outstretched arms, you would feel it for sure.

Friction from the air starts being detectable sooner than you might think. Have you ever stuck your hand out the window of a moving car? You noticed a feeling pushing on your hand, a feeling that increased the faster you went. This is sometimes called "wind resistance," but the more accurate term is drag. What you are experiencing with your hand out the window is the start of what makes it possible for airplanes to fly. Manipulating the way that air moves over, under, and around an object is what generates lift, making the air itself hold things up while in motion. When you set an object in motion through the air, it will be affected by drag in a variety of ways.

Unless you act to keep your object in motion, drag is a force strong enough to slow that object down and eventually bring it to a halt. The larger the surface that must be pushed through the air, the more energy it takes to push it, and the greater the effect of drag. If you have your hand out the car window vertically, the feeling of pushing on your hand is quite strong. If you turn your hand over flat so the narrowest part of it is hitting the air first, the push is lessened.

Quite a few things affect drag in the air, and one of these is the surface of your object. Anything rough, loose, or flapping will have a big impact on your aerodynamics. This is why bicycle racers not only ride bicycles that are made as smooth and aerodynamically sound as possible, but also dress in close-fitting, smooth-surfaced clothing and choose helmets with specially designed shapes intended to minimize drag.

Drag is always acting on your spindle to slow it down, and as you spin yarn and store it on your spindle, the mass of stored yarn (or cop), method of winding on, and method of securing your yarn will all play roles in how strong drag's effect is on your spindle's behavior.

The Yarn Being Spun

Mechanical engineers who design rotating objects consider all of the aforementioned factors, but most of them are designing objects whose shape will stay fairly constant while in action. That's not the case for spindles: when you wind spun yarn onto a spindle, many of its rotational dynamics change, because the shape, weight, mass distribution, and balance all change through time while you spin.

When you store yarn on your spindle, it gets heavier. It happens gradually, but it adds up over time. How you shape the cop of spun yarn and where you concentrate its weight can vary, but no matter what, your spindle will always become more center-loaded as it becomes heavier. This is because you store your spun yarn on the shaft and initially close to the axis of rotation. You're adding mass and increasing weight, adding it close to the shaft.

As the cop grows, it will grow up or down the shaft as well as outward. As your spindle gets progressively loaded with spun yarn, it gets more center-loaded both in terms of mass

distribution up and down the shaft and balance around the shaft. Ultimately, the cop will become the biggest factor in the spindle's behavior—far outweighing the properties of the unladen spindle. Yet even this isn't the biggest way in which the yarn you're spinning affects your spindle's behavior.

yarn dynamics

When mathematicians, engineers, and physicists study the torsion pendulum example, they're usually trying to find ways either to treat the string from which the weight hangs as massless and not really there or to eliminate torsion from the equation. What is this "torsion" that is so undesirable? It's exactly what handspinners are all about: twist. The reason that it gets left out in a lot of theoretical rotational dynamics is that it is actually very tricky to calculate and work with mathematically.

The simplest way to explain twist is to say that it is energy. It is the rotational force we're generating when we spin our spindles. We are harnessing it in the yarn we spin. We use it to turn loose fibers into yarn, and we also store it in the yarn. While we are working with it, it's not fixed in place—it can (and does) move, and how it does so has a wide range of results, some desirable, some not.

If scientists working with a torsion pendulum concept are using a suspending cord that has mass, then that cord affects how the pendulum behaves: how thick that cord is, how long it is, how dense it is, how regular it is, what materials it is made from,

and how those react to being used to store twist. These factors are hard to describe and explain in scientific terms, but by contrast they are absurdly simple in handspinning terms.

Simply put, a thicker and denser yarn has less capacity to hold twist and twist energy than one that is thinner and less dense. A shorter yarn can hold less twist than a longer yarn. Some fibers can accept more twist than others. Once yarn reaches its maximum twist capacity, no more twist energy can be stored in those fibers, and the twist must escape. It will attempt to do so in one of at least four ways: by moving out into new fibers, by forming "ply kinks" or knots with reverse twist (like a plied yarn), by breaking the fibers in your yarn so twist can escape, or by causing the suspended object—the spindle—to reverse its rotation and go back the other way.

If you are spinning a thick yarn, you will reach that yarn's maximum twist capacity much sooner than if you are spinning a thin yarn. Therefore, you need fewer twists per inch in a thicker yarn than you do in a thinner yarn. This means that the twist in the yarn will push back sooner, and it'll also push back harder, because each individual twist is bigger and has more pushing power (more stored energy). For a thicker yarn, you will generally want to choose a spindle with a higher moment of inertia. To keep putting twist into thicker yarn, you need more oomph. You get that from a heavier spindle.

The notch in this low-whorl spindle makes it easy to use suspended, but the pointed bottom allows it to spin supported.

spindle mass and yarn energy

Because thick yarns need fewer twists per inch, you'll also be affected by how fast that twist is moving as it goes from the spindle into the yarn. If it's moving very fast, it might be a challenge to draft fast enough. This may result in your shorter length of yarn filling up with twist before you're ready to allow twist into the new yarn. So where does it go? Back out to the spindle, making it slow, stop, or even reverse. A faster-spinning smaller spindle may be harder to use for spinning a thicker yarn, so you want a spindle that will tend to stay in motion but rotate more slowly—a spindle with its mass concentrated farther from the axis of rotation, or a rim-weighted (though rim-loaded is really a more accurate term) spindle.

It stands to reason that the opposite would also be true—that to spin a thinner, higher-twist yarn, you would prefer a lighter, more center-loaded spindle. For many spinners this is absolutely the case, but it's a complex question. Many experienced spinners can spin yarns anywhere from very thick to very thin on a larger spindle. On the other hand, you will rarely (if ever) find a spinner who spins very thick yarn on a small, light spindle.

In general, it is easier to make a larger spindle do a wider range of jobs than it is to make a smaller spindle multitask. If you have a large, heavy spindle that's fairly center-loaded, it can spin quickly, so you could use it to spin thicker yarn if you draft fast or thinner yarn if you draft a little slower. The same is true of a large spindle that's rim-loaded, because even though it's slower, you can just slow down your drafting. But it's hard to make a small spindle with a high enough moment of inertia—enough oomph—to keep generating twist when confronted with a thicker yarn.

What does this mean for you? If you're spinning on a very small (or lightweight) spindle that's backspinning quickly or just won't get started spinning, you can either seek out a larger spindle or spin finer. If the twist is moving too fast and you're having trouble drafting fast enough, you may want a more rim-loaded spindle. If your yarn is drifting apart from too little twist, you may want one that is more center-loaded. If your spun yarn keeps snapping, you may be putting in more twist than the yarn can handle or using a spindle that's a little too big or heavy for what you're trying to do.

As you gain skill with the spindle, you'll likely find you can override or work around many of these considerations. For example, many handspinners who start out spinning suspended switch to a supported-spinning mode when the spindle becomes heavily laden with yarn, by resting the pointed bottom tip of their spindles on a surface so some of the load is taken off the forming yarn.

Human Interaction and Other Factors

Spindles behave differently depending on physical factors and how they're used, but for most spinners, the single most important element in whether or not a spindle works for their purposes is less tangible. It's how you use the spindle: where it fits into your lifestyle, your personal ergonomics, your skill level, and your feelings.

Most spinners who have reached a level of comfort with spindles have a variety of spindles and choose different spindles for different tasks and situations. For example, if I plan to spin while walking outside, I generally choose a sturdy, medium-mass low-whorl spindle. I know it will be less likely to be upset by a strong wind or if I accidentally kick it while I'm walking. I can use it to spin a broad range of yarn and to store a fair amount as well. A tiny top-whorl spindle is less suited to this because it's more vulnerable to external forces like wind or jostling (at least until it has some spun yarn stored on it to change its mass).

How you set your spindle in motion, what kind of yarn you want to spin, what space you spin in (on the sofa, walking around, riding on the bus)—these will interact with the physical properties of your spindle in complex ways, all of which are bound to be factors in your success and your preferences. That's exactly as it should be! It's up to you, and there is no simple set of rules.

Thick yarn reaches its capacity for holding twist sooner and pushes back against the spindle's rotation harder than thin yarn.

WHAT ABOUT THE WHEEL?

Imagine a world where every inch of yarn for every purpose—clothing, tools, building, weapons—is spun by hand. Does the spindle leap to mind for you first or does the wheel? Even handspinners don't often stop to think about fifteenth-century Spanish explorers setting out on epic voyages in ships rigged with handspun sails or the mummies of Egypt being shrouded in spindle-spun linen. We read ancient tales like Homer's *Odyssey* and hear of Penelope, pressed to marry again in Odysseus's decades of absence, who promises to do so when she finishes her weaving, but every night she undoes the work she did all day, so her weaving is never done. We think of her weaving, but not of the spinning that had to happen first, with spindles.

Throughout most of human history—tens of thousands of years—all yarn everywhere was spun on spindles. Even today, much of the world produces yarn with spindles. The spinning wheel as we know it now, with bobbins and flyers, has only been around for a few hundred years. The oldest known variants (driven spindles such as great wheels and charkhas) are 1,500 years old at most. For most of history, in most cultures in the world, it would not be the wheel that would spring so quickly to mind as the primary implement for spinning, but the spindle.

History gives us plenty of undeniable proof that people can spin huge amounts of yarn with spindles. We know they can, because they did.

The spindle is undeniably a common starting point for many spinners. It's a low-cost, low-risk way to find out whether or not you're even interested in pursuing the act of spinning your own yarn. Once you know you'd like to keep spinning, it's also common to "move on" to a wheel.

Probably the single biggest factor driving the decision to switch to wheel spinning is a desire for greater productivity. Simply put, you want more yarn, and you want it faster, and the conventional wisdom (along with many spinners!) will tell you the wheel is the way to achieve that goal. But is that universally true?

Type of Yarn and Fiber

What fibers you're interested in spinning and what kind of yarn you want to create can lead you to choose a wheel or a spindle for a given project. To spin yarn that requires a lot of twist or fast-moving twist, it may be hard to find a flyer wheel that can keep up. It may be hard to find a wheel you can tune comfortably for spinning very fine, short-stapled fibers. It's no coincidence that the wheel wasn't widely adopted in places where those are the most common yarns.

Remember the physics of rotating objects? There are similar considerations dealing with spinning wheels. Detailed and excellent explanations of these can be found in Alden Amos's *Big Book of Handspinning,* but we'll talk about two basic categories of wheels: the driven spindle, such as the great wheel or charkha, and the treadle-powered flyer wheel.

Driven Spindle Wheels

The simplest wheel features one larger drive wheel that is connected by a belt or cord to a smaller pulley. When you turn the drive wheel, that motion is transferred to the small pulley by the drive band. For each time the drive wheel goes around, the smaller pulley will go around more times. If the drive wheel is 20 inches in diameter, and the pulley is 2 inches in diameter, the drive ratio (the difference between those two sizes) is expressed as 1:10. For each rotation of the drive wheel, the pulley makes 10 rotations. If the drive wheel turns 50 times in one minute, the pulley turns 500 times, or 500 revolutions per minute (rpm).

With a driven spindle, the pulley is attached to a simple spindle, such as a spike. One hand turns the drive wheel, leaving the other hand to draft. The spinning action on such a wheel closely resembles that of some supported spindles: one hand keeps the spindle in motion while the other holds your fiber supply and drafts. In essence, it is the same process, but depending on the size and layout of the driven spindle, you may be able to spin a much greater length of yarn with a driven spindle than a hand spindle, and it is simpler to keep the driven spindle turning at a constant, and very fast, rate of speed.

This driven spindle adds a great deal of twist very quickly, making it ideal for spinning short-staple cotton.

The bobbins on this flyer can be exchanged when full, and the treadle-powered pulley continues rotating without a hand to turn it.

Bobbin-and-Flyer Wheels

The bobbin-and-flyer system, combined with treadle power, presents significant changes from spindle spinning, whether with a driven spindle or a handspindle. The fundamental skills necessary to produce yarn with such a device no longer include yarn management; the bobbin-and-flyer arrangement handles that for you. Instead of keeping a spindle in motion, controlling the moving twist, drafting fibers, managing the fiber supply, and storing spun yarn, your hands need only control twist, draft, and manage your unspun fiber. Since you treadle with your foot (or feet), you have two hands free to draft, so you have a much wider range of drafting methods available with the flyer wheel than with the spindle wheel. Since bobbins are removable and interchangeable, you can hand off your spun yarn to someone else and get back to spinning on another bobbin—handing the next person down the line a package of yarn from which they can work immediately.

All of this means it becomes possible to produce a larger quantity of yarn with a smaller investment of time in learning physical skills. On the face of it, this would seem to make the spindle spinner (and the great wheel or charkha spinner) obsolete. The extent to which that happens, though, depends a great deal on what type of yarn you need to produce, from what type of materials.

Remember that a rotating object with a lot of mass concentrated far away from the axis of rotation will be harder to move—harder and harder, the faster it goes. The shape of what goes through the air is also a factor because of drag. For these reasons and several others, the bobbin and flyer arrangement encounters some limitations in terms of how fast it can feasibly rotate. Those limitations mean the rate of possible twist generation goes down.

In general, it is difficult to make bobbin-and-flyer wheels generate twist as fast as driven spindles or even handspindles. There's a point at which the advantages in yarn management may not be as significant if you're spinning very high-twist yarn or fibers that require fast-moving twist to become yarn in the first place.

Further, if your culture already supports and sustains extensive knowledge of spindle spinning (whether in hand or driven) and you already have spindles and spindle wheels, retraining for new skills and acquiring new equipment is less appealing.

Bobbin-and-flyer wheels came into their own for spinning long-stapled flax, which requires lower twist, and for spinning thicker wool yarns, such as those commonly used by twenty-first century knitters. In many cases, the spindle still remained the tool of choice for producing fine smooth yarns more popular for weaving. Economist Adam Smith is said to have estimated the productivity of British spinners as doubling with the advent of the Saxony wheel in the mid-1500s. The wheel was absolutely ideal for production spinning the yarns that were in demand at the time, and the subsequent greater availability of those yarns had a huge impact on the types of fabrics available and thus people's uses of fabric.

At this stage, the only things left to automate about spinning yarn were fiber preparation and drafting. It was almost two hundred years more before mechanical solutions for those problems were found, and once they were, they became factory-produced commodities, not things people made for themselves. But in the meantime, although Europe's production of fine flaxen and thicker or heavier-weight wool yarns had expanded thanks to the flyer wheel, almost all fine yarns and fabrics were imported to Europe from other parts of the world, specifically Asia and the East Indies, where such textiles were still produced with handspindles, driven spindles, and reeling systems for silk.

Because practically everyone in the English-speaking world (and much of Europe) has been accustomed to buying these goods from far away for centuries, they've lost the routine skills needed to produce them—skill with the spindle, for example. That's less true of cultures in which the spindle (including the driven spindle) never lost its foothold. In those cultures, we still see tremendous skill

and great productivity with the spindle, and the image of handspinning doesn't heavily feature the flyer wheel.

Handedness

When we build equipment for a specific goal, we tend to generalize about how that equipment will be used and who will use it. This is particularly true if we're producing the equipment in a non-custom way, so that it has interchangeable parts. Consider a walking wheel (another term for a great wheel): there's only one way you can set most of them up, with the large wheel on the right side and the spindle on the

left—which means there's only one side of it that you can stand on. You use your right hand to turn the drive wheel, which means you must use your left hand to hold your fiber and draft—a huge change from the spindle, where you can simply switch hands at will.

The downside is that you can't keep the spindle in motion if you aren't keeping a hand turning the drive wheel. This makes it prohibitive to use any two-handed drafting method with a driven spindle of this type, which narrows the field for the type of yarns you can spin.

Masters of the supported spindle tend to take very quickly to the driven

To operate this great wheel comfortably, the right hand must turn the wheel while the left hand drafts.

spindle; the drafting method is largely unchanged, and you can often get much greater speed and a longer length of yarn before winding on. Similarly, masters of the great wheel or charkha take easily to the supported spindle.

Yarn Storage

With a driven spindle, you still store your yarn on the spindle. Some such wheels have removable spindles, and you can fill up several and then work directly from them to ply; however, for many wheels of this type, it is still necessary to wind off from the spindle in order to work with the spun yarn further. Spindle-based skills, such as winding on and building a cop of spun yarn that stays neatly where it's placed, remain relevant with the driven spindle.

The other major type of wheel, almost always treadle-powered, features an arrangement called a bobbin and flyer system. First appearing as a concept in the late fifteenth century (found in da Vinci's notes in 1490), this setup gained widespread favor starting in the middle 1500s. Building on the spindle wheel, the spindle becomes an axle shaft to which a device called a flyer is mounted. Inside the flyer, a free-spinning bobbin also rests on the axle shaft. Bobbin and flyer can turn in sync or separately, and this mechanism is manipulated to cause spun yarn to wind onto the bobbin in a relatively automatic manner.

YARN IS SERIOUS BUSINESS

The global economic forces of the eighteenth century both affected and were affected by the developing textile mill industry. The British East India Company, founded in 1600, provided the economic backbone of the British Empire by trading in textiles and commodities such as indigo, saltpeter, and tea. European textile production at the time did not include fine cotton and silk, which came from Asia and the East Indies, as they had throughout most of history.

Entrepreneurs in what is now Great Britain developed their first textile mills in hopes of decreasing that dependence on foreign production of fine yarns and fabrics. During conflicts with France in the 1700s, successful blockades of East India Company ships (among other factors) diminished the effectiveness of that company's centuries-old global monopoly in the textile trade.

When fine cotton and silk became difficult to get in England, mill technology was pushed to produce finer yarns for finer fabrics. Once these domestically produced textiles gained ground, the demand for imports of such goods also declined, and so did the finances of the East India Company.

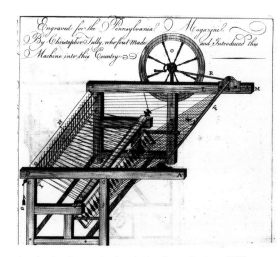

A spinning frame design dating from the late 1700s.

This decline in a major profit source for the Company was a factor in the creation of laws intended to protect and extend that monopoly. Laws were enacted to ensure that British colonies would produce raw materials, then ship them to England, from which they would in turn purchase finished goods. Most British colonies faced regulations against the local production of anything that the Empire wanted to make money producing, or that might lead too easily to self-sufficiency.

It was the goal to ensure colonial dependence and maintain the profitability of the British East India Company—England's financial powerhouse—by strictly controlling and taxing trade in both raw materials and finished goods. These sorts of regulations ranked high among the factors that gave rise to the American Revolution in the 1700s, followed by the revolt of other British colonies in the century to follow.

A spindle and fiber can go with you anywhere.

Lifestyle

Besides what kind of yarn you want to spin, how and where you want to spin it may cause you to choose a wheel for one job and a spindle for another.

Most wheels live in fixed locations. You can't walk around while you spin on a wheel; you set it up where it's going to be used and stay there while spinning. If you go pick up the kids from school, you have to leave your spinning behind. You can't take it with you while you walk the dog or use it on your commute to work. Even portable travel wheels are meant to be used while sitting in one spot—they are just easier to take from place to place.

Even inside your home, wheels take up a dedicated space, or else they require time to set them up and put them away every time you spin. The difference between a wheel and a spindle is a little like having a desktop computer or a laptop: A desktop computer probably lives on a desk, and when you use it, you sit where the computer is. Your laptop, on the other hand, could be used on the sofa, the kitchen counter, the deck—or taken with you to the coffee shop. A laptop is small and contained enough to use even in cramped quarters.

Spindles are essentially setup-free. Even moving that laptop around the house often means taking it out of its bag, plugging it in, and starting it up. A spindle is more like a pad of paper with a pen sitting by the phone, which you could use to take notes or doodle. Imagine if you picked up your spindle while on the phone instead of doodling. You'd be amazed what can happen in three to five minutes with a spindle, and you'd be amazed how much those small chunks of time can add up.

For spinners who live in close quarters, it may not be feasible to commit dedicated space to hobby equipment. A wheel can take up a lot of space! There are modern wheels that fold up very small for storage, but sometimes just finding the space to set up and spin can be a challenge.

Cost can't be ignored either. While luxury artisan spindles do exist and are a delight to use, even these are generally substantially cheaper than even entry-level wheels. Functional spindles can be bought (or made) for the price of one trip for fast food or fancy coffee.

Spindles are for the most part maintenance-free, and very little can go wrong with them. While it's possible to break a spindle, it's usually easy to tell what happened and whether it can be fixed with ease. Most things that can go wrong with a spindle are not hard to fix or work around. For some people, the mechanical aspect of spinning wheels makes them harder to understand and therefore less accessible.

For most spinners, sitting down at the wheel is a commitment of time. It can be hard to make that statement, even to ourselves—we may say the same things about spinning that we might say about going to the gym: "I just can't find the time. I don't know what I'd do with the kids. I only have about half an hour between getting the chores done and bedtime and by the time I get set up there's no time to do anything."

Plenty of modern spinners who have a wheel (or multiple wheels) have lots of spindles on which they'll have a variety of projects going, ready to pick up at a moment's notice. Wheels and spindles are not mutually exclusive by any means.

I also use spindles for sampling. If I'm going to shop for fibers, I like to have a spindle to test something before I buy. I always have a spindle or two next to my carder in my studio so I can test blends I'm developing.

Don't Leave Home Without One

There's a spindle and fiber in the bag I carry when I go out—okay, and I admit there are emergency spindles and emergency fiber in my car. This stood me in good stead when my car broke down and I was stuck waiting for assistance. I tend to keep inexpensive spindles around that I can give away in case I unexpectedly meet someone who needs to be taught to spin.

How often does that really happen? More than you might think; if you spin in public, sometimes folks are curious about what you're doing. It's wonderful to be able to teach them a bit and give them a tool they can take with them.

For those who knit or otherwise craft in public, spindle spinning can be a delight. Once you're up to speed with it, spinning takes less mental focus than a lot of knitting, and there's pretty much no risk you'll skip a row in your pattern, miscount, or get home to realize you have to rip out all the work you did while you were out. It's easy to spin and talk,

and almost any point can be a stopping point within a few seconds.

All of these elements combine to make spindle spinning a very approachable pursuit: it can be done inexpensively, in small chunks of time stolen from a busy schedule, in little space, anywhere you happen to be. It's a low-risk pastime with limitless potential and a rich history that's as old as human civilization itself.

Lifestyle is probably the most common reason why contemporary spinners in the modern world find themselves choosing spindles over wheels, but it's not the only one.

This three-stranded ball can be plied on a spindle while walking around, talking on the phone, or waiting in line.

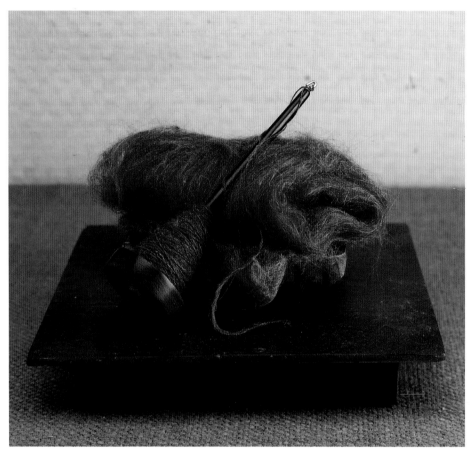

When using a spindle, it's easy to bring the yarn to eye level.

Ergonomics

Whether you're spinning yarn for your own enjoyment or producing it for a living, you don't want it to hurt. The tools we use, and how we adapt ourselves to them, have a huge impact on how we perform tasks with those tools. Wheels are more restrictive than spindles in several ways. There is a more limited range of positions you can be in to operate a wheel than to use a spindle. The size and layout of a wheel will determine how you have to sit (or stand) to work with it, which in turn will determine the range of angles at which you can be drafting. The combination of those factors will have an impact on what kind of drafting methods you can comfortably use.

What if you're spinning a fine or delicate yarn that's hard to see at arm's length? When spinning with a wheel, it can be awkward to bring the yarn up close to your eyes to look at. You may be tempted to hunch over to get a closer look—not comfortable for the long haul and potentially a limiting factor if you're spinning very fine. With a spindle, on the other hand, you can draft within inches of your eyes, with your drafting zone at any angle, in any plane. This is one reason why spinners who use both wheels and spindles often find they can spin finer with spindles than with wheels.

Hand Position

On a wheel, your forward hand (the one closer to the orifice) is typically palm up in your lap. This means your drafting zone crosses the palm of your hand starting at the pinkie side and ends with thumb and forefinger serving as a gate for twist coming from the orifice of your wheel. If you are accustomed to spinning this way, the parts of your hand that are used to feeling for twist and controlling it, are likely the surfaces of your thumb and index finger that face each other if you lay your hand flat palm down on a table.

To see this for yourself, put your fiber supply hand in your lap, palm up. Now put your forward hand in front of it, also palm up. Notice that the thumb and index finger side of your fiber supply hand is closest to the pinkie side of your forward hand. Turn over your forward hand so that thumb and forefinger are closest to the thumb and forefinger of your palm-up fiber supply hand. With your hands in your lap, this is the only way you can have the thumbs and forefingers closest to each other.

If you're spinning at a wheel and you want the thumb-and-forefinger parts of your hands to be closest to each other, the only comfortable way is by turning that forward hand over so it's palm down. This means you either can't get a good look at the yarn you've just formed or you must hold the other three fingers on that hand out of the way somehow. You could either splay them out in another direction or curl them under, almost like a partial fist. This isn't comfortable, and your production rate and consistency will both suffer.

There are also changes in the mechanics of drafting because of the greater range of possible motion with a spindle and because the spun yarn can be manipulated further by your fingers while still in clear view. Think about it this way: if you're drafting with a two-handed method on a wheel, your drafting zone passes over the palm of your forward hand. If you were to bring in your other three fingers toward your thumb, you would be touching the fibers being drafted. On a spindle, though, you'd be touching the yarn you have just spun. For spinners accustomed to using all of their fingers, the obstacles a wheel poses to doing so can be limiting.

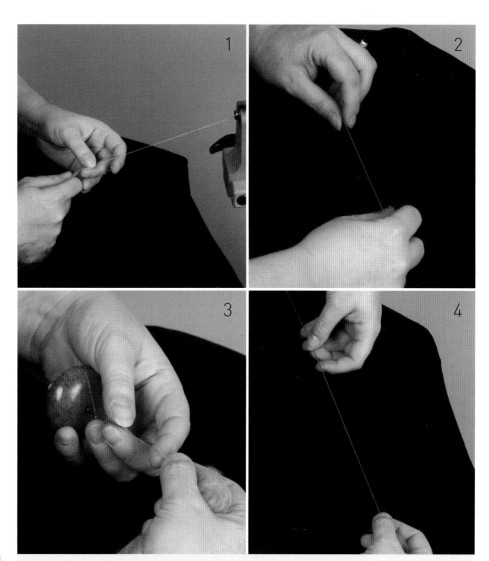

hand-position ergonomics

1 A spinning wheel almost forces your hands to be in one position: palms up, with the pinkie finger of your drafting hand closest to the index finger of the fiber hand.

2 Placing both of your hands palm down is the most comfortable way to bring the most sensitive and dexterous fingers of both hands together.

3 This hand position is natural and comfortable on a spindle but difficult on a wheel.

4 It's easy to use all of the fingers on your drafting hand to fine-tune your spun yarn on a spindle.

The whorl of this spindle is made of moose antler.

Why Spindles?

With these limitations, how did the wheel take over from the spindle in so many cultures? Why do so many contemporary spinners produce a lot more yarn with a wheel than they do with a spindle?

One factor is the types of fibers available. In regions where the predominant fibers are very fine (such as silk) or very short in staple (such as cotton and animal downs), the spindle continued to provide advantages over the flyer wheel in particular. The flyer wheel as we have known it for several centuries excels at producing large quantities of yarn quickly from coarser or longer-stapled fibers, and in a setting where people work at set tasks in a fixed location more than they incorporate textile production into the spaces around other daily tasks. Climate is likely a factor in this as well, as long cold winters give people in some areas more time where being indoors is absolutely necessary—so sitting beside the fire with a spinning wheel isn't such a hardship.

Another factor is cultural. If you have a problem to solve, some cultures will tend to approach that by coming up with a set of procedures for handling it, while others will tend to devise a tool instead. Neither approach is inherently superior, but there may be contexts in which one is more effective than the other. If your procedure takes a long time to learn or requires practice to perform, then it can only be done by people who have been trained to do it. If you don't have the method, means, and time to provide that training, you'll probably be happier with a tool, and you may benefit from reducing your dependence on skilled labor.

This leads right to a third reason: the learning curve. Although regarded as a beginner's tool in the industrialized world, the truth is that production spinning with a spindle requires lengthier training and more practice than production spinning with a wheel. The ramp-up time for churning out a steady volume of yarn with a wheel is less than for doing so with a spindle. In most cases, you can turn someone into a good wheel spinner more quickly than you can turn someone into a good spindle spinner.

Either way, a spinner must be able to draft and manage twist. With a spindle, you must also be able to generate the twist, keep it coming or decide to stop it, and perform all your yarn management manually. The wheel allows you to eliminate some of those considerations. If you can get the hang of treadling or turning a wheel with one hand, then you no longer have to worry about paying attention to how fast your twist is moving or whether it might suddenly turn around and go backward. Add in the interchangeable bobbin concept, and the flyer that automates a majority of your winding-on worries, and you've removed a lot of formerly necessary skills. Instead of needing a spinner who has been trained up from childhood to produce at a certain rate, you can train adults to do it in a matter of months. There's a much broader pool of those, and you can have them on short notice.

Textile Automation

This sounds a lot like discussions of modern-day workforce automation, and that's no coincidence. It's the same thing; and the production of textiles was the first major task to be automated at the dawn of the Industrial Revolution. Being able to devise machines that reduce the training required to produce large quantities of goods changes everything in a civilization's lifestyle. Every step toward automation makes the next step possible. Changes in what people must do on a daily basis to survive become permanent very quickly—in as little as one generation. Once they have, it's difficult to go back or to find ways to incorporate no-longer essential skills into our routines.

The spinning wheel is a brilliant device, and it absolutely allows for more production sooner . . . for yarn within its range. In turn, the availability of such yarn changes what people expect to do with it. You start to find uses for the yarn you can produce the most of, which creates more demand for that yarn. Bit by bit, this reduces demand for the stuff you can't produce as quickly without extensive training, and the demand for the people with that training diminishes, too, resulting in fewer of those people, and the training disappearing. Dependency on the tool-based solution increases, and in the larger picture, the tool-based solution—the spinning wheel—becomes most productive because there's nobody left who can produce in great volume without it.

It takes more time to become a productive spindle spinner than a productive wheel spinner, but once you leap that hurdle, the skills that make you fast with the spindle make you much faster with the wheel than you would otherwise be. In the modern world, the wheel and spindle aren't mutually exclusive—in fact, they coexist quite nicely.

A wide variety of yarns is possible with spindles.

Spinning on a Spindle

Although the physical characteristics of a spindle can make a difference in how it performs, the biggest factors are determined by what you do as a spinner. From your first yarns to production spinning, this chapter talks about how to use your spindles.

STARTING TO SPIN

Once you've chosen a spindle or two to start with, it's time to get down to business. Let's start by selecting fiber for our first efforts.

While it would be appealing to say there's one right fiber to start with, the truth is there isn't. Spinners the world around and throughout history have started with all kinds of fiber. If there is something you're specifically drawn to, chances are it's a good choice. But if that isn't working out for you or you want a jumping off point given the wide range of fibers presently available, here are a few suggestions.

You may have a ready source of fiber that you're interested in spinning. Perhaps you are learning to spin in order to make yarn from your own animals or you're interested in spinning cotton you've grown. Maybe you are inspired by gorgeous handpainted fibers or can't wait to try cashmere.

These things are all terrific, but if you're spinning for the first time, they might not be the fastest road to success. Most spinners find that the quickest, best results come from well-prepared, undyed medium wool that is carded, not combed.

If you are unable to find carded fiber, choose commercial combed top that has not been dyed. (Dyeing can compact fibers and make them handle differently, and that's not a great starting point.) You want to start out with fibers that don't need any extra work or fiddling to get them to spin. That's the same reason why you might not want to start right out with your bunny's fur or your first alpaca shearing from your flock.

Buy plenty of fiber. If you can, err on the side of having too much; think how sad it would be to get the hang of it and have to stop because you're out of fiber! Start with at least 4 ounces (115 grams), and preferably more. It will probably be gone before you know it.

Pick several types of fiber and a variety of preparations to try. If one fiber frustrates you, there'll be something

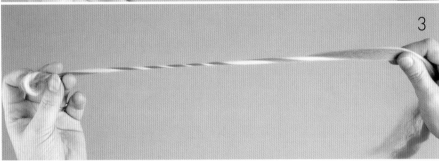

how to **twist fiber into yarn**

1 Fibers can easily be tugged apart and will even separate completely.

2 Tug apart carefully so the fibers don't come all the way apart.

3 Twist the fiber between your hands by twirling your fingers.

4 With twist added, the fiber is too strong to be pulled apart, and you have yarn!

else on hand to try immediately. Coopworth, Romney, Corriedale, and Bluefaced Leicester are excellent wool choices for a new spinner.

These are general guidelines. If you can't resist spinning something from your flock, then go ahead! It's never a bad idea to start out with fiber you really want to spin (unless you will be heart-broken if it doesn't become exactly the yarn you envisioned on the first try). The more you want to spin something—the more you feel it calling to you—the more likely you'll be to practice and the faster you will learn.

How Does Spinning Work?

Spinning is simply the act of tugging fibers apart while introducing twist to them, so that they hold together.

Spinning with a Stick

You don't even need a spindle to make yarn—just take a length of fiber, stretch it out a bit, and twist it. Once you can do that, you can create an unlimited length of yarn, but how do you store that yarn neatly while you're creating it? One good solution is the stick—you can simply wrap your yarn around a stick.

The stick itself can help twist the fibers. Just by wrapping the yarn around the end of the stick, pulling it off the side, then wrapping it more, you can insert twist faster, meaning you can make yarn in less time and store it right on the stick. You can twirl the stick in your hands and make the fiber twist up. You can pull against the fiber while it's twisting, and now you're making yarn very quickly indeed.

The more yarn you build up on the stick, the heavier it gets, and the more it tends to stay in motion when you twirl it. It will keep twirling even if you drop it—even faster than if you're just turning the stick in your hand.

Children in the Andes start learning to spin as soon as they can sit up and grab things by wrapping fiber around a stick. When you hold the stick steady and move your hand to wrap the yarn, every wrap you make goes around the end of the stick instead of straight on from the side. This results in one twist per wrapping motion, and that's enough to make a thick yarn by itself.

Be careful to pull from the side; if you pull off the end, you will take out all the twist you just put in. You can see the same effect with a roll of party streamers or paper towels: Place the roll on the ground and stand above it. Take hold of the end and pull up. For every wrap that comes off the end of the roll, you will get a twist in your streamer. But if you pull the streamers off the side, the paper will stay flat. Coming straight off the side doesn't add twist or subtract it; the same is true when we're talking about yarn.

The spindle is an extension of these principles that has led to a broad range of yarn-making tools.

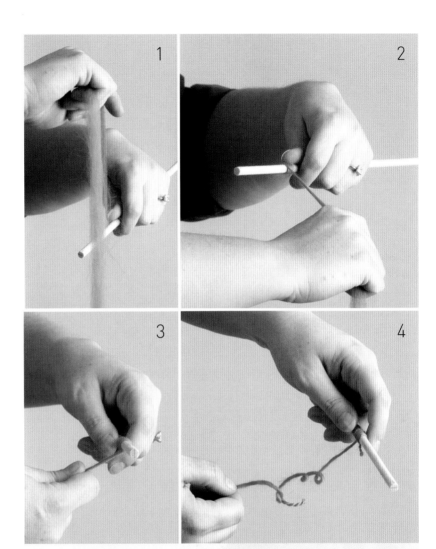

how to **spin with a stick**

1 Hold one end of a length of fiber on a stick and place your other hand about 6" (15 cm) out along the fiber, pinching tightly.

2 Use the hand holding the fiber to wrap it around the stick. Do not let go with the tightly pinching hand.

3 Without letting go of the fibers you're pinching, twirl the stick so you can gently pull the fibers off toward the side of the stick.

4 Your fibers are now twisted into yarn. Twirl your stick and wind the yarn on from the side to store it.

Repeat Steps 1–4 to see the twist build up in your yarn.

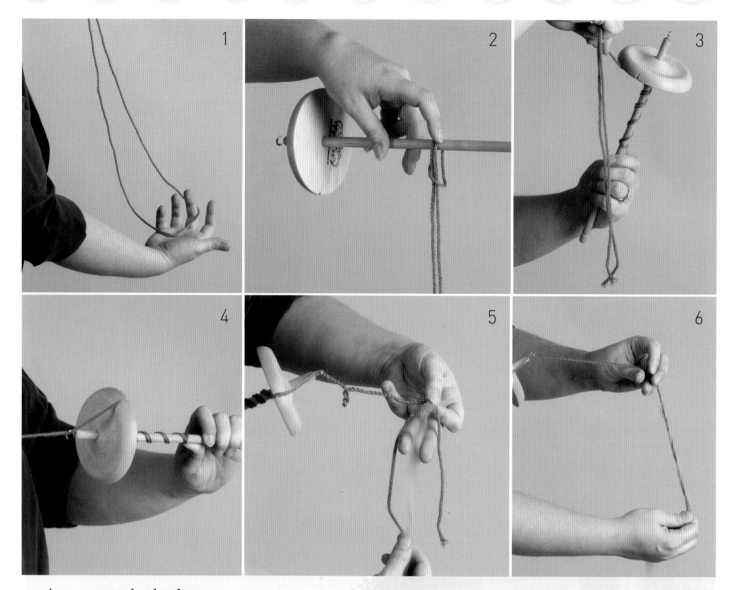

how to **attach a leader**

1 Cut a piece of yarn 1 yard (1 meter) long and fold it in half.

2 Place the looped end behind the spindle shaft and draw the two ends through the looped end and around the spindle shaft.

3 Pull tight and wrap both strands of leader a few times around the spindle by twirling the shaft.

4 Secure the leader (which is 2 strands) to the top of the spindle. This may be a hook or just the top of the shaft, depending on the type of spindle. Leave 8–12" (20–30 cm) of yarn coming off the spindle.

5 Attach fiber to the leader by placing it between the 2 strands of doubled-over yarn.

6 Twirl the spindle in your hand to insert twist in the fiber, and you're ready to go.

Meet Your Leader

The portion of yarn between the spindle and your hands when you start the spindle is called the leader. "Leader" can refer to a pre-spun piece of yarn you use to get started or to the portion of yarn between your spindle and your hands when you're starting to spin a new length. Many spinners find it easiest to get started using an already-spun yarn as a leader. This may be especially true if your spindle does not have a hook.

Attach a Leader

A leader in this case is simply a piece of already-spun yarn attached to the spindle used to start spinning fiber (see directions at left). One thing that may make this trickier—and may make you move away from pre-spun leaders as you gain skill with your spindles—is that after you have attached the leader, you must then attach the fiber to the leader.

Spin a Leader

If your spindle has a hook and you are comfortable with drafting (pulling fiber apart while adding twist), you may prefer to use the hook to spin your own leader (see directions at right). Don't worry about making the yarn perfect or exactly as you plan to spin the whole batch.

Making a Half-hitch

Although some spindles feature hooks, notches, or other devices for securing the yarn to the spindle, they're not

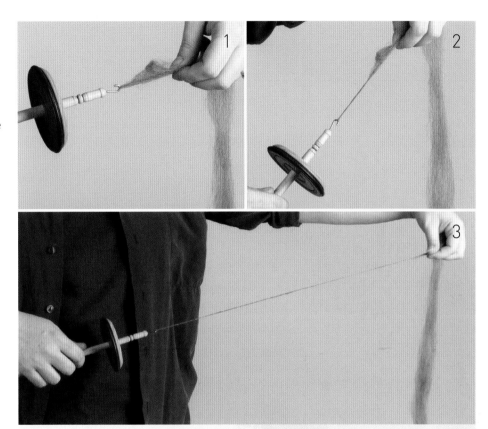

how to **spin a leader**

1 Fold over a few of the fibers you're about to spin and catch them with the hook.

2 Holding the spindle in your hand, twirl it to generate twist in the caught fibers.

3 Pull back on the fibers gently and let more twist run into them. Continue adding twist and drafting out yarn for a foot to a yard.

strictly necessary with many spindles. A simple half-hitch is reliable and, with a little practice, can even be much faster than working with hooks and notches (see directions on next page).

If you are not confident in your half-hitches or your yarn or spindle is slippery, you may wish to use more than one half-hitch. Spiraling the yarn up the shaft makes even multiple half-hitches easy to undo, and they simply vanish into thin air when removed from the spindle's tip.

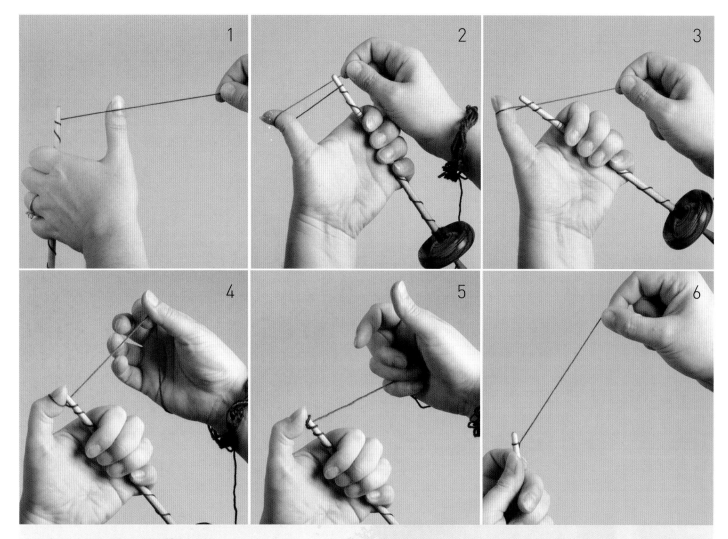

how to **make a half-hitch**

1 Spiral your spun yarn around the spindle shaft up to about a finger's width from the tip. Hold the spindle with your fingers and place your thumb under the yarn.

2 Move your thumb up to form a loop and bring that loop to the side of the spindle shaft.

3 Cross the yarn over the yarn coming off the spindle.

4 Place the tip of your thumb on the tip of the spindle's shaft.

5 Slip the loop of yarn on your thumb off onto the shaft.

6 Pull the loop tight, and your half-hitch is complete. When you need to remove the half-hitch, it will slip off easily because of the extra yarn stored by spiraling up the shaft.

Park and Draft

Now that you have fiber attached to your spindle, you are ready to spin. This can be harder than it looks—especially if you've been watching someone who is good at it.

Spinning is a physical skill; you may understand in your head, but if your hands don't know the motions, it's not easy. To learn, your hands need a chance to understand the process. Park and draft is a good way to do this.

With park and draft, there are three steps: creating twist, drafting, and winding the yarn onto your spindle. These will become one fluid process, but when you're starting out, it helps to break them up into steps.

This technique is used by beginners, but experienced spinners use it, too.

Add Twist

Hold your spindle in one hand by the leader portion of yarn, pinch the yarn before it gets to the unspun fiber, and don't move those fingers. Keep the yarn pinched right between spun yarn and unspun fiber. Flick the shaft with your fingers. Watch closely to see twist going into the spun yarn and make sure the spindle keeps spinning. If it slows down and wants to backspin, catch it with the hand you used to flick it and hold it. You're just piling up twist in the leader.

Check your leader to see how twisty it is; you want to see it super-twisty, even kinking up on itself. (If it isn't that twisty, flick it again.) You're still holding the leader yarn and keeping it pinched, not removing that hand that's separating the leader and the unspun fiber (although

they're connected). That pinching hand is like a floodgate keeping the twist from moving into your unspun fiber. You're trying to stockpile a lot of twist in the leader. The leader is acting like a twist battery, holding on to it until you are ready to distribute it.

The twist is potential energy, and it wants to go somewhere. Yarn can only hold so much twist before that twist wants to get out. While you're spinning with a spindle, it can only go in two directions: out into your fiber supply or back toward the spindle. If it goes out into your fiber supply before you are ready, it can lock up your fiber and make it hard to pull it apart (see page 59). If it goes out toward your spindle, it will cause your spindle to turn in the opposite direction and make your yarn

how to **park and draft**

1 Pinch between the unspun fiber and the spun yarn.

2 Flick the shaft of the spindle to add twist.

3 Stop the spindle as soon as it slows down and starts to backspin.

  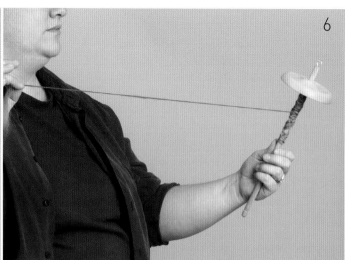 

how to **park and draft** (continued)

4 Park the spindle between your knees so it can't move unexpectedly. Check that there is plenty of twist built up in the leader. Move the hand that was flicking the spindle up to the hand that was pinching.

5 Draft out some of the unspun fiber until it is about the diameter of your desired yarn. The area between your hands is called the drafting zone. Slide the pinching hand up over the drafted unspun fiber.

6 Wind the yarn onto the spindle by twirling the shaft.

7 Leave enough spun yarn for a leader.

When you have practiced this and get the hang of it, you will likely find that you move to spinning without parking, without even realizing it. This leap takes most new spinners anywhere from one to six weeks.

unspin itself. Because you don't want either of these things to happen, keep those pinching fingers right where they are. Now you have to find a way to keep the spindle from spinning the wrong way, so put the spindle between your knees if you are seated or tuck it under your arm if you are standing. (This is the "park" of "park and draft.")

Once you have the spindle parked so that twist can't escape, move the hand that flicked the spindle up next to the hand pinching off the twist (on the leader side). It's going to take over the job of pinching off the twist.

Draft

Let go with your fiber-supply hand. Using your now-free hand, gently tug fibers apart. Don't pull them apart completely, but just until they are thinned down into what seems like a good amount of fiber to have in your yarn. (Just wing it! Don't worry if it's not perfect.) This is the "draft" of "park and draft." If you are having trouble getting the fibers to slide apart, try moving your hands farther apart and tugging over a greater distance. Your hands are probably just a little too close together, and moving them apart will make drafting possible.

Now that some fiber has been drafted, let the twist into it. Gently slide the fingers of the pinching hand along your drafted fibers. You will be able to feel the twist that you stored up in your leader moving with you back into those fibers. The result is yarn.

Keep drafting fiber and allowing twist in until you have as much yarn as you can manage or until you run out of stored twist in the leader. (Stop drafting when the leader stops kinking up.)

Wind your newly spun yarn onto your spindle, leaving 8–12" (20–30 cm) for a new leader. Repeat the whole process.

COMMON PROBLEMS

Most new spinners run into a predictable set of problems, and without a little guidance they can seem like huge obstacles.

fibers won't tug apart

HANDS TOO CLOSE TOGETHER

Most of the time, you just need to move your hands a little farther apart. The individual fibers are only so long; this length is referred to as the staple. If your hands are closer together than the individual fibers are long, then when you try tug the fibers apart, you may be tugging on both ends of the fibers, which keeps them from sliding past each other.

TWIST IN THE FIBER SUPPLY

Twist is like glue; it wants to stick your fibers together. If they are already twisted, it will be difficult to slide them apart. The twist may have totally locked up your fiber supply, turning it into yarn—yarn the thickness of your entire fiber supply. The twist will move through as much fiber as there is for it to touch. To solve this, let your fiber supply dangle loose in the air hanging from the yarn you have already spun. If it starts twisting around on its own, you have twist in your fiber supply that is making its way out. Once it stops moving, try again.

PROBLEM FIBER

See if you can tug it apart at a point away from the spindle—just grab a piece and see if it comes apart. If it doesn't, you may want to try different fiber. If it moves, but only with a lot of effort, try loosening it up with your hands. Just pull and fluff it with your fingers until the fibers seem more willing to move, then try spinning again.

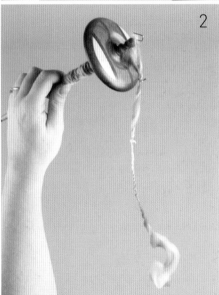

twist in the fiber supply?

1 Twist in your fiber supply can prevent the fibers from drafting.

2 Let the fiber supply hang loose so that the extra twist can run out.

Twist Tips

* The thinner your yarn, the more twists it will need in every inch in order to hold together as yarn; the thicker it is, the fewer twists per inch it will need.

* Are you going to ply your yarn (twist several strands together to make a stronger yarn)? If so, remember that it will lose some twist when plied. What you think is a very twisty yarn may not be that twisty once it is plied. This is another good reason to err on the side of too much twist if you aren't sure what the right amount is.

thick spots and thin spots that you don't like

IT'S NORMAL

While you are getting a feel for spinning, don't worry if it's thick and thin. If you absolutely can't stand it, you can go back over those thick parts and draft them out thinner; see page 68.

yarn keeps breaking

SPINDLE TOO HEAVY

Your spindle might be too heavy for the thickness of yarn you are trying to spin. Don't thin down your fiber quite as much to create a thicker yarn.

TOO MUCH TWIST

You may be putting in so much twist that the fibers become stretched to their limits and snap. Try storing less twist in your leader before you start drafting.

spindle stopping too soon or backspinning

YARN TOO THICK (OR SPINDLE TOO LIGHT)

You may be trying to spin a thicker yarn than your spindle is suited for. Try switching to a heavier spindle (which will be better at working with thicker yarn) or thinning your fiber more to spin a finer yarn. You may think thinner yarn won't be strong enough, but you might be surprised how strong yarn really can be.

leader too short?

1 This leader portion may be too short to store enough twist.

2 This leader portion looks long enough.

LEADER TOO SHORT

Try leaving a longer leader portion. 8–12" (20–30 cm) is usually plenty, but even that is a wide range. If you don't have a long enough leader, then the "twist battery" effect doesn't work because there isn't enough room to store much twist.

yarn drifts apart

YARN TOO THIN (OR SPINDLE TOO HEAVY)

You may have better luck spinning thicker yarn, especially if your spindle is on the heavier side.

NOT ENOUGH TWIST

You need more twist in your yarn. Don't worry if it kinks up on itself a bit; this is normal and it will come out in the wash (or in plying). Also don't worry if your yarn seems too wiry and stiff. When you're just starting out, I believe you're better off with too much twist than too little. Yarn with more twist will hold together, while yarn with less twist might come apart—if not now, then when plying or using it. It's easier to fix a yarn that is twistier than you want than one that drifts apart from having too little twist. To get more twist in your yarn, store up more twist in your leader before

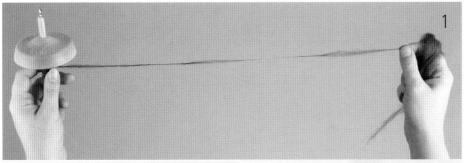

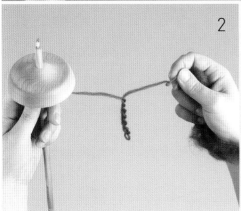

not enough twist?

1 If there isn't enough twist, the yarn will drift apart.

2 The yarn should have enough twist to kink up against itself.

a lot of that twistiness will go away. Don't judge your yarn until you have skeined and washed it or until you have plied, skeined, and washed it. This is a normal. Don't expect your yarn to look from the very beginning the way you envision it to knit, crochet, or weave. It still has a way to go before it's ready for that.

can't make yarn at all (and you're tempted to use the spindle to start the grill)

CHANGE IT UP

Try some different fiber or your other spindle. You may need to change things up a little to let your body really learn. What works for one person doesn't necessarily work for everyone (or anyone!) else. It's okay to experiment and find ways that feel comfortable to you. There is no single way to spin.

you start drafting, or stop drafting now and work on getting more twist in before you proceed.

yarn kinks up on itself

TOO MUCH TWIST

You may have more twist than you really want, but it's going to take time to know for sure. If you have a few corkscrews and pigtails, don't panic.

JUST RIGHT FOR WASHING OR PLYING

You're better off with a very twisty yarn than a yarn that isn't twisty enough. Once you have skeined and washed your yarn,

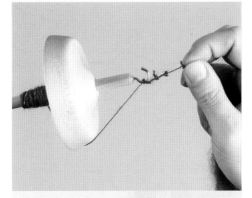

very twisty yarn?

Yarn that corkscrews and pigtails isn't necessarily a cause for worry.

TIME FOR A BREAK

If you're just plain frustrated, it's okay! This actually is harder than it looks. Remember, the people who make it look easy have been doing it longer than you have. Give yourself a break—literally. You are learning a new physical skill, and you need to give it time to sink in. For most new spinners, 15–30 minutes a day for a few weeks is enough. At some point, if you keep trying when you're already frustrated, you're not helping yourself improve.

The Spindle Is Full— Now What?

After you've spent a while parking and drafting, you will have piled up a bunch of yarn on your spindle. You may wonder, "How do I know if my spindle is full?" There are several ways to look at this, but the simplest answer is that your spindle is full if you feel like it is.

Here are a few common tip-offs that you may have put as much on your spindle as you want to:

* It's heavy and awkward to manage, although it wasn't before.
* It's hard to set it in motion at all—it hurts your fingers to flick it or you can't get it up to speed.
* Your cop of spun yarn is getting unwieldy; there isn't enough shaft left for you to grip it comfortably or wind on any new yarn, or the cop wants to slip off.
* The yarn you're spinning keeps breaking because the spindle is now heavier than the yarn can support.
* You can't spin the same yarn as you did before because the spindle has gotten heavier.
* Your spindle is performing differently from how it did early on in a way that you don't like.

We'll talk more in Getting More Done about ways to maximize the amount of yarn on your spindle, how to get longer skeins of finished yarn, and your personal productivity with the spindle. For now, if your spindle is so full of yarn that you aren't comfortable with it or you can't keep spinning the same yarn, then you've got a spindle full of yarn.

So now what do you do? You have to get it off to use the yarn (or to use the spindle to spin more yarn). How do you do it?

Wind a Ball

You can do this with a ball winder or nøstepinne if you have one, you can wind around something like a tennis ball, or you can wind a ball by hand. Wind your fresh singles tightly to store them under tension, so they can't tangle up just sitting in the ball. I wind my yarn into a ball if I'm going to spin more yarn and ply it (see page 101 for plying information).

Tie a Skein

You can do this with a niddy-noddy or a skeinwinder if you have one, or you can wind it around your arm or a good-sized sturdy book. I wind a skein if the yarn is to be used as singles or if I'm taking plied yarn off the spindle. Always tie your skein in at least two places and preferably more.

how to **wind a ball**

1 Spread your fingers a bit (so winding yarn on them doesn't compress them uncomfortably). Hold the end of the yarn against one finger with your thumb. Wrap the yarn around your fingers ten to twenty times.

2 Pull the wrapped yarn off your fingers. Grasping one end of the loops you wrapped around your fingers, wrap more yarn around the middle of the loops.

3 Fold this in half and wrap more yarn around the outside; you may be able to repeat this step several times.

4 Continue wrapping, turning the ball periodically as it grows.

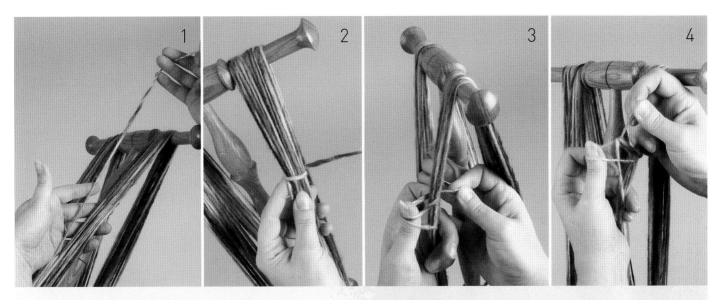

how to **tie a skein**

1 Hold the end of your yarn and grasp along the loops of the skein, leaving at least 8" (20.5 cm) of yarn to tie with.

2 Wrap the end of the yarn around the part of the skein you're holding in your hand.

3 Stick your thumb into that wrap to keep it from getting too tight, and wrap one more time.

4 Pass the yarn end through the two loops and pull tight to secure it. Make sure it holds and doesn't slip around.

Finishing Yarn

Once you have a skein of yarn, you will generally want to wash it (unless the yarn is a novelty structure, you want to work with it in its unwashed state, or if you know the materials in the yarn won't take well to water). For most fibers, I wash my yarn in a basin of hot water with a mild soap, then rinse it in cool water.

I like to dry yarn by simply hanging it to dry with no weights and not under tension, but some people prefer to weight or block their yarn. I prefer the yarn to show me its true character at this stage of the game before I use it in something. However, if I know it's going to be hard to work with because it's very twisty, I might weight it. One easy way is to take a bag with handles and put something heavy (like a can of soup) in it. Then slip the handles over a coat hanger and place the coat hanger at the bottom of the skein to weight it while it dries. You can add or remove weights in the bag easily.

Once your yarn is washed and dried, use it for whatever you like! You may want to hold on to your very first skein of yarn so you can look back at it throughout your spinning career and always have that memory of what it was like starting out. Others like to make it into a special project and keep it that way. The choice is yours! Congratulations on your first handspun yarn.

Fine-Tuning your yarn

If you didn't have access to all kinds of fibers and tools, you would spin only the fibers that were locally available, using the tools that people in your area had developed to work with those very fibers. Spinners in ancient Egypt produced fine linen yarns for weaving; spinners in the Andes spin weaving yarn from camelid and sheep fibers; lace knitters in the Shetland Isles spun the fleece of their sheep into yarn for knitting shawls.

But you can spin almost anything with any tool, and you probably want to spin yarns for a wide range of applications. You don't need to specialize. This means there are fewer absolutes and more ways to approach a goal.

This chapter won't give you a long list of things you must do in a particular way to get a long list of specific results. Instead, let's understand what forces are in play and what tools you have available to control the yarn you're spinning. It's up to you to decide on your yarn goals and to forge your own path—even if your goals change or if you want to achieve multiple ends.

The major things to understand and manipulate are the thickness of your yarn, how much twist is in it, and how dense or lofty it is. If you can control these things, you can put them all together to make a near-infinite variety of yarns.

With a modern wheel, spinning thicker or thinner usually involves changing settings on your wheel. With a spindle, the changes you make to spin different thicknesses of yarn aren't so obvious. You could simply change spindles, and in many cases that's all it takes, but there is more to the picture.

Drafting Methods

How your fibers are prepared and the method you use to draft them are major factors in controlling loft and density. A worsted preparation is one in which all the fibers are aligned parallel, such as in combed top; a woolen preparation is one in which they're arranged more randomly and pointing in multiple directions, such as in carded roving or rolags.

Woolen and Worsted

There are as many ways to draft as there are spinners, but we tend to categorize them in one of two ways: either a worsted method (in which twist only enters fibers after they have been drafted to the desired thickness) or a woolen method (in which twist plays an active role in your drafting and is actually in your drafting zone). Worsted methods such as short forward draw or "inchworm" produce denser, smoother, drapier yarns, while woolen methods such as one-handed long draw produce fuzzier, loftier, lighter weight yarns.

Different fibers call for different kinds of preparation and different spinning methods. Fibers with a very long staple length (such as long wools, alpaca, or flax) are best prepared and spun worsted, while short-staple fibers (such as cotton or cashmere) are best prepared and spun woolen. But there's a lot of middle ground where it's possible to mix and match styles of preparation

woolen draw

1 In woolen spinning, twist is allowed into the drafting zone.

2 The fibers are drafted apart between the hands as the twist forms them into yarn.

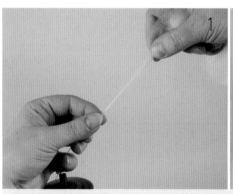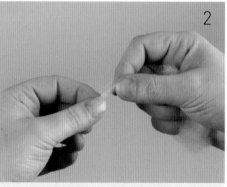

worsted draw

1 In worsted spinning, the hand closest to the spindle pinches off twist, keeping it out of the drafting zone.The fibers are drafted out between both hands, which have no twist between them.

2 The hand closest to the spindle slides closer to the fiber hand, allowing twist into the drafted fibers and smoothing them down.

and spinning, producing yarns that are neither pure worsted nor pure woolen. Most contemporary spinning falls into this middle ground, and the nuances of the woolen-worsted spectrum are a subject of seemingly endless debate in the spinning community. For our purposes, when we talk about worsted spinning, we're talking about drafting methods that use both hands and keep twist out of the drafting zone; when we talk about woolen spinning, we're talking about methods with twist in the drafting zone.

how to **double draft**

1 To begin a double-drafted pass, draw out a long section of fiber between your hands.

2 Pull your hands apart gently to attenuate the fibers until you have a length as long as you feel you can manage comfortably; this is the woolen first pass.

3 Wind the partly drafted yarn on your fingers to "walk" the yarn back to the beginning of the pass. (Add more twist by spinning the spindle as needed.

4 Starting at the spindle, tug and smooth each length of partially drafted fiber between your hands. You will need to keep the spindle in motion during this process because thinning down the yarn will require more twist; if the spindle stops moving, you may run out of twist and find your yarn drifting apart.

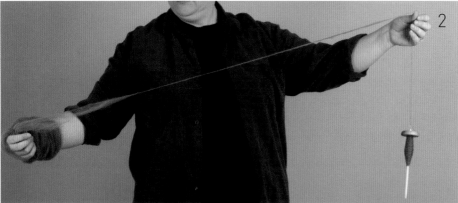

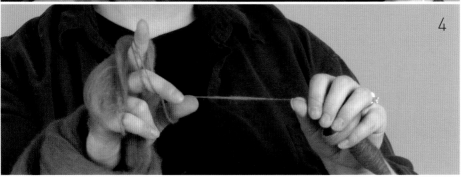

Double Drafting

Double drafting is a technique that mixes elements of woolen and worsted drafting methods. It consists of an initial long draw followed by a second pass on the same drafted fibers, during which you fix every slub and produce a smooth, even yarn. Double-drafting methods can tend either to woolen or worsted, depending on that second pass. Double drafting usually works best with airy carded fibers.

While woolen and worsted are terms that describe specific yarns in a historical context, they're also useful as the English terms defining the ends of a spectrum of possible yarns. Fiber selection, style of preparation, and method of drafting are tools you can mix and match to create exactly the yarn you desire. In between these ends are an infinite number of possibilities—and different spinning traditions include many different takes on these generalities as well. The more time a spinner spends thinking about woolen and worsted, the more questions he or she is likely to have. Relax! This is normal—it's one of the most hotly debated topics in the spinning world today.

Consistency

When you started spinning, you probably made lumpy thick-and-thin yarn. Controlling your drafting to make a yarn of consistent thickness is the first hurdle to overcome. But since mastering that, you may have found that your yarn gets finer and finer, and then it's hard to spin thick again.

Why does this happen to so many spinners? A lot of it is a result of learning to spin more consistently. When you encounter a slub, you want to break it up and thin it to be like the yarn around

it. There is no obvious way to make the yarn on either side of the slub thicker, so the immediate solution is just to draft out that slub. But another factor is that it really is trickier to spin consistently thick than consistently thin.

When you are spinning with a worsted draw (where twist does not enter your drafting zone), most spinners find it easier to micromanage everything. You pull out only the number of fibers you need from your fiber supply. Before you let twist turn it into yarn, you make sure the fibers are all exactly how you want. Then you gradually ease twist back into your drafted fibers and start the process over, pulling out the same number of fibers from your supply again.

Removing Slubs

Sometimes you get more fibers out in your drafting zone than you really meant to, and you just can't seem to make them thin down enough. This can happen due to the preparation of the fibers or the nature of the fibers you're spinning, but another common reason is letting a little bit of twist sneak in there.

fiber slub

To eliminate a slub that occurs due to the nature of the fibers, the best solution is to pick the problem fibers out and start spinning again (unless that slub is a yarn design choice).

twist-locked slub

Dealing with a twist-locked slub is a little trickier. Remember when I said that the primary cause of fibers not drafting is having your hands too close together? With a twist-locked slub, the twist in the yarn on either side of the slub effectively does the same thing. There are two ways to break it up: by moving your hands farther apart on the thin parts on either side of the slub and tugging; or by getting right into the center of the slub and breaking it up. Initially, you may find this easiest to do if you park your spindle so it can't backspin on you while you work your slub.

When you break up the slub, twist will move from each end toward the middle as the fibers thin down. The more fibers you have in your yarn, the fewer twists per inch that yarn will hold. A twist-

how to **remove a fiber slub**
1 This slub is due to the preparation of the fiber.

2 Remove undesired slubs from your yarn by pinching them and pulling them right out.

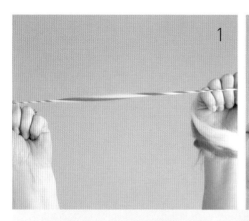 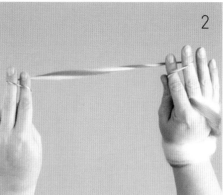 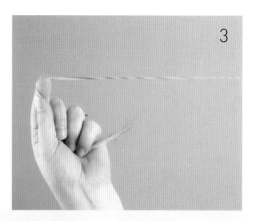

how to **remove a twist-locked slub**

1 This is a twist-locked slub. Both the thick slub and the thin parts on either side are full of twist and prevent further drafting.

2 Grasping either side of the slub, use your fingers to untwist a little so the slub can be drawn out.

3 As you thin down that fiber, some of the twist from thinner areas of the yarn will run in. You may need to start spinning again to add twist so the thinner yarn doesn't drift apart.

locked slub is essentially a piece of very thick yarn surrounded by thinner yarn on both sides. As you thin that slub down, it needs to get twist into the new, thinner yarn to hold together; you may need to add a little more twist to the whole length of yarn afterward.

You may have so much twist in the yarn on either side of your slub that you just can't make it move, no matter what you do. If this is the case, take a moment to be thankful you're spinning with a spindle, because taking twist out of your yarn is really easy with a spindle as compared to a wheel. Simply spin the spindle in the opposite direction for a few seconds, until you can tug that slub out and draft it down to the thickness you desire.

THINNER, THINNER, THINNER . . . OOPS!

When I was a little girl learning to spin, one of the problems that took me the longest time to overcome was a tendency to spin thinner and thinner yarn. I was so captivated by the magic of a little bit of gossamer forming and holding up a spindle that I would think about little else. Maintaining the same thickness throughout an entire spindle was an enormous challenge. One good way to overcome this is by setting aside a small sample (a length of spun yarn) from the beginning of your spindle to refer to as you spin more. Wrap 10"–12" around a stick or a card to keep it under tension. From time to time, check what you're making against that sample. If it is no longer comfortable to match it, it may be time for you to wind off.

Default Yarn

Although inconsistency may be a big problem at first, you may find that before long you have the opposite problem: no matter how hard you try to spin differently, your yarn remains stubbornly consistent.

By the time you're comfortable with the processes of spinning (which could be as little as a month or two), you have probably developed muscle memory that will lead you to produce the same yarn almost no matter what you set out to do. Spinners refer to this as "default yarn"—what you tend to produce when you aren't even thinking about it, or what you quickly switch back to if you become distracted. There's nothing wrong with this, but you should know that your default yarn is trainable, perhaps most so when you're relatively new to spinning.

Muscle-memory defaults tend to develop most rigidly for specific tools. It's not uncommon for a spinner to have one default yarn with one spindle and a completely different one with another. If you are having trouble shifting your habits, trying a different tool, a different fiber, or both, may be all it takes to break you out of a rut.

In the long run, being able to spin lots of different kinds of yarn takes practice and time. The more different things you try, the more your hands will learn. Developing muscle memory that lets you produce a default yarn from one type of fiber doesn't mean it will immediately translate to success with another. Each new fiber or tool that you pick up may have its own learning curve, and that's normal.

Twist

Deciding how much twist you want in your yarn is subjective, and the answer depends on many factors. Do you plan to ply your yarn? If so, you'll want more twist than if you plan to use it as singles because plying removes some twist from the singles. What is the yarn's intended purpose? Higher-twist yarns wear better and are generally less prone to pilling; however, they are usually not as soft to the hand (though generally soften a great deal in the finished object). What are your materials? Longer-staple fibers don't require as much twist to hold together as yarn and may feel increasingly harsh if spun with high twist. Shorter-staple fibers need more twist, and if they're spun with too little, they may pill unacceptably even if the yarn holds together.

There's no magic formula for the exact right amount of twist; you'll need to decide that for every yarn. But there is a simple way to tell if you have too much or too little twist: If the yarn just drifts apart, you don't have enough twist. If it kinks up and snaps when you try to pull the yarn straight, you have too much. Anywhere between those two ends is structurally sound yarn, and it's up to you to decide where you want your yarn to fall on that spectrum.

Measuring Twist

Some spinners like to measure the amount of twist in their yarn by counting the number of twists in an inch of spun yarn. This is fairly effective, but the thinner your yarn, the more twists it will have, and the thicker the yarn, the fewer. There is a more dependable measurement: angle of twist (measured by holding the yarn against a protractor). The angle of twist will stay the same regardless of the number of twists per inch, and this can be a more consistent measure of how much twist is in your yarn, regardless of how thick or thin (or even variable) it is.

The number of twists in an inch can still be relevant, however, so it behooves a spinner to be able to measure both.

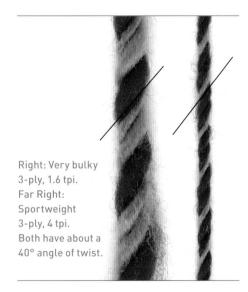

Right: Very bulky 3-ply, 1.6 tpi. Far Right: Sportweight 3-ply, 4 tpi. Both have about a 40° angle of twist.

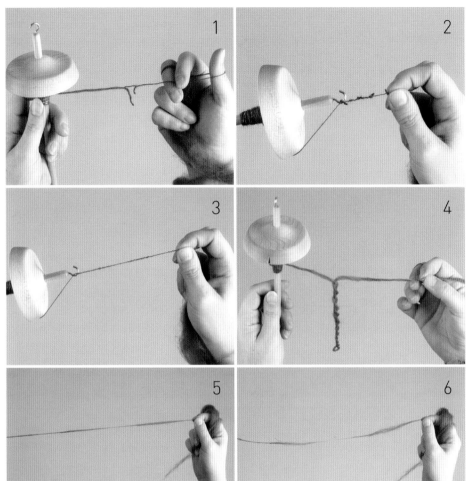

how much **twist?**

1 A freshly spun singles will always twist back on itself. This is normal and desirable. Yarn will twist back on itself at the thinnest points by default.

2 Singles with too much twist will form corkscrews that cannot be pulled out straight without breaking the yarn. This is hard to do with a suspended spindle because this much twist will usually cause backspin before you reach this point.

3 You can fix too much twist by drafting out more fiber and allowing that excess stored twist to move into it.

4 Freshly spun yarn can twist back on itself even if it doesn't have enough twist to really hold together.

5 If your fibers still slip past each other and allow further drafting, your yarn does not have enough twist yet.

6 If your fibers are not twist-locked, the spindle will not bear their weight; your yarn will drift apart, and a suspended spindle will fall.

Fiber Choice

The type of fiber and drafting method affect the weight and shape of spindle you are likely to prefer and even whether you want to spin supported or suspended.

No matter what tools you use to spin, the relationship between twist and yarn diameter is always present. However, some fibers fill up with twist sooner than others, and some fibers will not become stable as yarn until they have more twist. This means that the type of fiber you're spinning can also affect the spindle you will want to use to spin it.

In general, the longer a fiber's staple, the less twist it will require in order to be a cohesive yarn. By contrast, if the fiber is shorter in staple, more twists per inch are needed for structural integrity. This helps determine how quickly you want twist to get into your fibers and thus how quickly you want your spindle to generate twist. The properties of the fiber also affect your choice of drafting method.

Diameter and Twist Control

Controlling the thickness of your yarn is inextricably linked with your ability to control twist. The ability to spin yarn at the diameter you want depends on your ability to make twist be where you want, when you want, in the quantity you want.

In other words, one fairly straight-forward way to change the diameter

how do we achieve that with spindles? One way is to choose a different spindle. Different sizes, weights, and shapes of spindle behave in different ways. The faster your spindle spins, the faster it will generate twist. The longer it spins, the more time you have to draft before you must either wind on or restart the spindle. The greater the spindle's moment of inertia, the more twisting power the spindle will have in general.

This is the major reason why some spinning teachers recommend starting with a heavier spindle with a high moment of inertia. That spindle is easier to keep in motion than a lighter one, until you gain the muscle memory to make drafting adjustments on the fly. It's also a reason why rim-weighted spindles are popular: they have a strong tendency to keep rotating, usually combined with a slower overall speed of rotation. This tends to be the most forgiving (and in the long run the most flexible) of spindle choices.

Another way to change the rate of twist generation is by changing the way you set your spindle in motion. Starting your spindle with a flick will almost always result in slower rotation than you get from starting by rolling. The exception to this is large support spindles, which can be rolled slowly and which are not left to rotate suspended (see page 91).

Drafting Speed

The next consideration in controlling the diameter and amount of twist in your yarn is managing drafting speed. When you started out, you probably couldn't

of your yarn is to change how fast the twist is moving. For example, if your spindle is rotating at a rate of 200 times per minute, it will generate 200 twists per minute. If you draft at a rate of 5 yards (or 180 inches) per minute, you'll make yarn that has 200 twists divided by 180 inches, or about 1.1 twists per inch. This can only be a thick yarn; a thin yarn won't hold together with only 1.1 twists per inch. If your spindle rotates at a rate of 1,000 rpm and you still draft 5 yards in a minute, you can get yarn with 5.5 twists per inch—which has to be a thinner yarn, because a thick yarn won't hold that much twist and will make your spindle backspin.

It may take a while to feel you have the control you want over the rate at which twist moves through your fiber as you draft. This is one reason why it's easier to get consistent at spinning finer than thicker. There are few absolutes in spinning, but one of them is that (assuming the same fiber) a thinner yarn requires more twists per inch than a thicker yarn. It's easier for yarn to absorb one or two extra twists per inch here and there if it has an average tpi of 20 than if it has an average tpi of 6; there is a smaller difference between 20 and 22 twists per inch than there is between 6 and 8. Going from 20 to 22 tpi might change your angle of twist by 10%; going from 6 to 8 could change it by 33%.

With a wheel, the rate of twist insertion is changed by going from a lower (slower) ratio to a higher (faster) one. But

draft very fast compared to experienced spinners (or how fast you'd become with practice). If you are spinning finer, there is less chance for twist to get ahead of your drafting than if you are spinning thicker. What's more, your hands are smarter than you might think they are. They may instinctively try to make room for all that twist that's coming into the yarn, and the way that is obvious to your hands to do this is by making thinner yarn, which can hold more twist.

If your yarn has so much twist in it that it feels stiff and unpleasant, try drafting your fiber out thinner as you spin. The thinner yarn, with the same overall volume of twist, will probably be more to your liking. This is an easier adjustment for most spinners to make than simply drafting faster. It's so easy that it often just happens, contributing to the problem of constantly getting thinner as you spin!

Conversely, if you find that you are spinning yarn that just drifts apart, your drafting speed is outpacing your twist, and you need more twist to make yarn hold together at that thickness. The easy answer is the opposite of the last one: don't draft as thin, and you'll make thicker yarn that's right for the amount of twist.

Faster-moving twist will generally require you to draft faster. Once you can draft quickly, you will be able to speed up and slow down in response to the way the twist is moving. There are several ways to control how fast your twist moves, but the most obvious ways are to choose a spindle that tends to spin faster or slower (something you will only be able to evaluate subjectively and by feel) or to change how you set your spindle in motion. But there is more to the picture! Perhaps, as a beginner, you started out with park and draft. Believe it or not, this can be an advanced technique as well.

Moving Twist

Remember that twist isn't set in stone as soon as it gets into your fibers. That's what makes park and draft work: you use the leader portion of your yarn like a battery that you charge up with twist while spinning the spindle and then deplete to fill up the fibers you're drafting while the spindle is parked. As a technique for beginning to spin, we usually focus on how this makes it easier to control because there isn't more twist coming at you while you're trying to draft; but as an intermediate or advanced spinner, it's a method of managing twist that lets you have more or less at a time than the tool you're using wants to provide by default.

In the long run, your hands will probably tend to perform the same tasks at essentially the same speed—neither as fast or as slow as you can possibly go, but somewhere in the middle. As you gain experience, your default drafting speed is likely to increase in response to being given faster-moving twist to handle. As your drafting speed increases, so does your level of control over the moving twist, and along with it the range of yarn that you can spin with comfort and confidence.

What Spindle Should I Choose for Which Fiber?

Spinners of longer-staple fibers (most wools or flax) and spinners using worsted methods will generally be content with medium to heavy spindles in a wide range of shapes. Spinners of short-staple fibers and spinners using woolen methods may have more exacting demands for a spindle and are likely to find that there are fewer variables that make for a spindle ideally suited to their purposes.

This isn't to say that you can only spin a given fiber with one type of spindle or one type of technique, but it's not a coincidence what types of spindles and related techniques have developed to deal with various fibers. As a contemporary spinner, you'll likely find some of these guidelines useful when selecting tools for your goals.

One way to think about how heavy a suspended spindle you want is by considering the weight of the fibers you intend to put on it in one cop. In other words, if you are looking for a spindle onto which you expect to spin 15 grams of superfine fiber into gossamer yarn, a spindle that weighs 15 grams is probably a good choice. If you want a spindle that will hold 2 full ounces of plied sock yarn, a spindle that weighs 2 ounces is likely to be ideal. This doesn't hold true for all spindle shapes and types, but for garden-variety suspended spindles, regardless of whorl placement, it works more often than it doesn't.

SPINDLE SELECTION MATRIX

This chart demonstrates how to break free from your default spinning by choosing a different spindle, a different fiber, or both. For example, if your default yarn tends to be high twist and you are using a center-weighted spindle, simply choosing a rim-weighted one instead will change quite a bit about your yarn.

YARN OBJECTIVE	SPINDLE CHOICES	DRAFTING METHOD	RATE OF TWIST INSERTION	WHYS AND WHEREFORES
Fine yarn from long-staple fiber	Very light to fairly heavy; center-weighted for fastest production, rim-weighted for longest spin time and slower-moving twist	Worsted, woolen, or double-drafted; combination and hybrid variants are also possible	Any!	If your spindle spins slowly, you will need to draft slower to get sufficient twist into the yarn or put in extra twist before winding on. Long-staple fibers don't need as much twist to hold together, so you have a lot more wiggle room.
Fine yarn from short-staple fiber	Very light, unless supported; center-weighted for fast spin	Typically woolen or double-drafted	Moderate to fast	Shorter-staple fibers need more twist to hold together, and you have to get that in there fast if spinning suspended. (If spinning supported, you don't need to get the twist in as quickly because the yarn doesn't need to bear the weight of the spindle while forming.)
High-twist yarn from any fiber	Weights vary, but center-weighted is the most common choice	Worsted, woolen, double-drafted, and other specialized or hybrid draws	Fast	The more twist you are looking for, the faster you will want to get it in there.
Low-twist yarn from any fiber	Medium to heavy and rim-weighted for suspended spindles; very large and usually heavy for supported	Worsted for most yarns, very occasionally woolen for extremely thick yarn	Slow to medium	If your twist is moving too fast, it will be very hard to draft fast enough to stay ahead of the twist while keeping the yarn low in overall twist.
Thick yarn from long-staple fiber	Fairly heavy to quite heavy, and rim-weighted, if suspended; very heavy if supported	Worsted or extensively predrafted	Slow to medium	Thick yarn requires less twist to hold together; if the twist moves too fast, it is hard to stay ahead of.
Thick yarn from short-staple fiber	Medium weight to heavy if suspended; typically heavy if supported	Worsted, extensively predrafted, or slubbed woolen	Slow to medium, but usually faster than with long-staple fibers	Thick yarns require lower twist, but short-staple fibers also require more twist than longer ones.

The Right Spindle for the Job

For the contemporary handspinner who has access to any type of spindle and any type of fiber, you can choose to use the tools that developed over thousands of years with the techniques that developed with them, or you can mix and match to produce a truly limitless variety of yarns.

You are also likely to find that the skills that go with one type of tool complement others and may even transfer in ways that seem surprising. For example, if you are a very proficient spinner with support spindles, you may not find it hard to spin long-draw woolen yarns with a suspended spindle. There's no law that says you can only spin a given yarn with one type of spindle.

It's not only the type of yarn and fiber you want to spin that affect your choice of spindle. Sometimes how you plan to use the spindle will affect the kind of yarn you make.

A Matter of Taste

If you love a spindle, chances are you will use it a lot, right? But what if you love it so much you're afraid to ever drop it? Or what if it's beautiful but tiny and light, and you don't like to spin fine yarns? Maybe you used to enjoy the spindle but lately it just isn't the same. And what about spindles that everyone else seems to love, but you just don't?

Spindles are just like anything else: your tastes and moods and desires can shift over time, and there's no reason why everybody has to like the

same things. There are many reasons why a given spindle might or might not work for you. There are generalities, and it can be helpful to understand what elements may be contributing to your feelings about a spindle—but don't be afraid of simply having preferences for reasons you can't put your finger on. It doesn't necessarily mean anything about you as a spinner, any more than a preference for vanilla ice cream over chocolate does.

What if you don't like chocolate or vanilla—does that mean you just don't like ice cream? Maybe you've only tried ice cream cones, and you actually might really like eating it with a spoon.

It probably took you years to figure out your ice cream preferences, and spindles are no different. While you went through your lifelong process of developing specific tastes in ice cream, whether you realized it or not, you also developed a wide range of skills you now take for granted. Have you ever fed a small child an ice cream cone? Without fail, the child ends up with a lot more ice cream all over her than a grown-up would. You may have forgotten, but you learned how to keep ice cream from melting and dripping while you eat it.

You don't think about these processes as an adult, but you spent years learning them. You learned them hands-on, by trial and error, by observing what other people do, and by taking chances. The same is true for spindles: you will need to develop some skill with them and try lots of different things to know what really works for you.

getting more done

Even if you've fallen in love with spindle spinning by now, you may be wondering when you'll start making as much yarn on a spindle as you've heard is possible. This chapter covers ways for the brain and the body to maximize productivity. Understanding how to spin faster is easy; training your body in new movements is harder. Spinning is like playing a musical instrument: you may understand theory and read music, but being able to play what you see (and have it sound the way you want) still requires practice and physical skills.

Where Does the Time Go?

If you feel like you aren't getting enough done with your spindles, the first step is to evaluate where you're spending your time. Break up your spinning into a set of repeatable individual steps, then spin normally and time each of the steps in turn.

Are you surprised by where you spend your time? Most spinners are. Without consciously timing what you do, it's very hard (maybe impossible) to have an accurate picture of where your production bottlenecks really are. The four steps listed here are a good start, but you may have others, and surprising amounts of inefficiency can arise from other areas (such as managing your fiber while you spin). Some of those steps may prove unnecessary when you really stop to think about it, or you may be able to eliminate or minimize those complications.

Here's a common set of repeatable steps:
1. Set the spindle in motion.
2. Draft and spin a length of yarn as long as you can handle before winding on.
3. Wind the yarn onto your spindle.
4. Secure your yarn to the spindle (if applicable).
 Once you've finished Step 4, start over with Step 1.

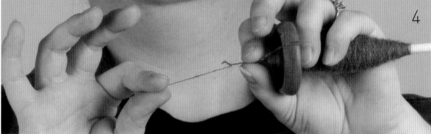

how to **time it**

Here's a common set of repeatable steps:

1 Set the spindle in motion.

2 Draft and spin a length of yarn as long as you can handle before winding on.

3 Wind the yarn onto your spindle.

4 Secure your yarn to the spindle (if applicable).

Once you've finished Step 4, start over with Step 1.

Complete the sequence 3 times and time it. (It may be easier to take turns timing with a fellow spinner.) Record each individual time and take the average; for our example, we'll use 103 seconds.

Now perform the sequence 3 more times, timing each individual step. Simply timing steps may be an eye-opener; where we think we spend our time and where we actually do can be completely different. Calculate your average times for each step. Let's say the average numbers look like this:

* Set spindle in motion: 5 seconds
* Spin a length of yarn: 40 seconds
* Wind onto the spindle: 50 seconds
* Secure your yarn: 8 seconds

Check to see if the total time for all the individual steps seems similar to your time for the whole sequence. If it doesn't, is there something you do in your whole spinning sequence that you didn't think to time? It's not uncommon to miss a step when you're thinking about what you do instead of working on autopilot.

Factors in Efficient Spinning

Greater efficiency usually means greater speed. Saving seconds here and there may not seem like much, but they can really add up. Using the example of our four basic steps and an average time of 103 seconds, a spinner could complete those steps about 35 times in an hour. If that sequence produces 1 yard of yarn, that's 35 yards in an hour. But if we could shave 1 second off starting the spindle, 3 seconds off drafting, 10 seconds off wind-on, and 3 seconds off securing the yarn, the spinner could produce about 42 yards an hour.

Time savings isn't the only type of efficiency. What if we couldn't shave any time off that 103 seconds, but we could go from producing 1 yard of yarn per wind-on to producing 1½? We'd produce about 52 yards of yarn in that same hour.

These numbers depend on spinning nonstop for an hour; in reality, we will probably have to stop during that hour. The only way to be sure is to spin for an hour and measure again. (See *The Alden Amos Big Book of Handspinning*, pages 172–173, for more on drafting, spinning, and production rates.)

Some spinners find their results over an hour are the opposite of what they expected. You might think you'd stop to solve some problem or get distracted and produce less, but people often find they have spun more than they expected. Athletes often find the same thing: the first lap isn't the fastest. You get faster when you have warmed up and hit your stride—things just start to flow. All physical skills are like that to a degree, and spinning is no exception.

That brings us to the final major element in spindle productivity: muscle memory. This is hard to describe because it can't be quantified. Have you ever heard it said that the hand is quicker than the eye? It's true—and it's also quicker than the brain. Muscle memory is what happens when your body knows how to do something without you thinking about it.

Although small changes in your technique can make a big difference in your production rate and there are lots of mechanical and systematic ways to be more efficient, nothing in the world makes a spinner faster than developing muscle memory for it. The only way to develop this is with time and training, just like an athlete, dancer, or musician. Well-trained muscle memory is what makes high performance possible in any physical pursuit.

That ability doesn't come overnight, but it is trainable with exercises and practice. Some obstacles to productivity can be solved by thinking them through (the brain stuff, if you will). Others require physical training. You can't use reason and understanding to solve these; they're the body stuff, and you get past these obstacles with practice.

Setting the Spindle in Motion

There are two major ways to set your spindle in motion: flicking and rolling. Flicking uses your fingers to make the spindle rotate and requires only enough shaft to fit your fingertips. Rolling uses both hands or one hand plus something else (like your thigh). To roll a spindle into motion, more shaft needs to be exposed (at least a hand's width) than to flick it. Rolling is usually hard to do if there is a hook, notch, or other type of catch on the part of the spindle where you need to roll; for this reason, rolling is more common with high-whorl spindles where the exposed shaft is at the opposite end of the spindle from the

This spindle features a carved swirl instead of a metal hook, and since there is one at either end, the spindle is completely reversible. Slip on the cover to protect the swirl on the part you aren't using.

hook, with low whorls that don't feature a hook or notch, or with large supported spindles that have plenty of exposed shaft simply because the spindle is so big. Flicking is more common with small spindles of all varieties, low- or mid-whorl spindles where the hook or notch is close to the exposed shaft, or if you're spinning in a small area.

flicking

If you look at it up close, flicking is similar to rolling: you roll the spindle's shaft between your fingers and thumb. You can flick the spindle at the top of the shaft, at the bottom, or anywhere along its length that you can get a decent grip.

Where rolling is a large and expansive movement, flicking is a small and subtle one. When watching other spinners, it's fairly straightforward to tell what they're doing when they roll: up or down the thigh, with which hand, and where their hand rests on the spindle shaft. But because flicking is such a small movement, it can be hard to tell what a spinner is doing when starting a spindle in motion that way.

When you set your spindle in motion by flicking, the motion that's easiest to use is the one that is most like snapping your fingers. If you snap-your-fingers flick with your left hand, your spindle will rotate counterclockwise, or S. If you do it with your right hand, you'll get a Z, or clockwise, rotation.

When flicking a spindle, the amount of spin you give it depends partly on how thick the shaft is where you flick. Flicking a thin, pointy tip will create faster spin than flicking a thick part. Practice flicking the spindle in various different places to see what different effects you get.

exercise FLICKING WITH A FINGER-SNAP

You can do this using a supported spindle or a suspended spindle, but a support spindle with a fine point and no hook works especially well for getting the movement down. If you

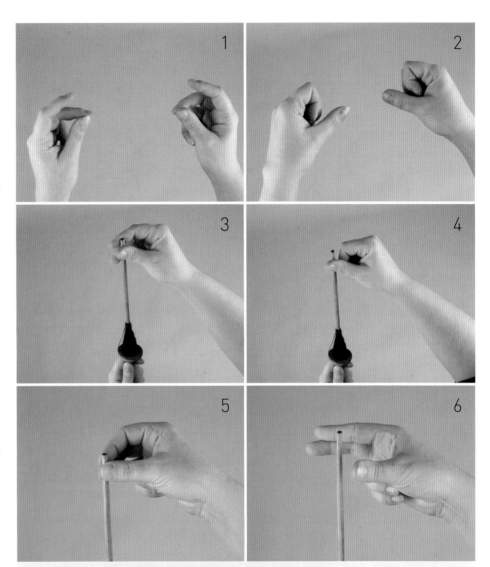

how to **snap or flick the spindle**

1 Setting a spindle in motion can be a lot like snapping your fingers.

2 You can also start a spindle with a flicking motion.

3-4 To flick a spindle clockwise with the right hand or counterclockwise with the left, hold the shaft between your first two fingers and thumb and snap your fingers back against the base of your thumb.

5-6 To turn a spindle counterclockwise with your right hand or clockwise with your left hand, use the same fingers to hold the spindle but flick your fingers forward instead of backward.

don't have a spindle that fits that description, you can use any relatively smooth stick, like a chopstick or bamboo skewer.

Rest the base of your spindle on any surface (even your lap) and hold the spindle loosely in the hand that won't be setting it in motion. Give it a little support so it stays roughly where it is and doesn't go flying. You aren't even going to be spinning, just working on making the spindle go. Put the thumb and index finger of your other hand at the tip and snap. Try it with your thumb and first two fingers, then with your thumb and middle finger. Snap as hard as you can.

With your other hand, feel how much twist is added, how quickly, and for how long the spindle keeps going. This is good to practice with both hands in each role! If you snap with your right hand, your spindle will spin clockwise (Z), or to the right. If you do it with your left, your spindle will spin counterclockwise (S), or to the left.

This builds finger strength and helps you determine what's the fast way for you to flick.

rolling

You will usually get the greatest speed and longest spin time from rolling, but rolling also requires more leader to temporarily absorb twist rapidly without backspinning while you get your hands ready to draft. Rolling is hard to do if there is a hook, notch, or other type of catch on the part of the spindle where you need to roll; for this reason, rolling is more common with high-whorl spindles where the exposed shaft is at the opposite end of the spindle

from the hook or with low whorls that don't feature a hook or notch. Rolling a suspended spindle works well for spinning yarn when you have plenty of space to work in because the movements are larger.

Your spindle's specific physical properties will have an effect on the speed at which your spindle's rotation stabilizes; a center-weighted spindle will tend to spin faster, while a rim-weighted one will tend to spin longer.

Because rolling is generally more forceful, it brings with it a few risks that are not as pronounced in flicking: Your stored yarn may come loose from the hook, notch, or hitch, and go flying out of reach, tangling your spun yarn. Fine or fragile yarn is more prone to snapping, as it may not be able to take the weight of the spindle suddenly. If your spindle is

not heavy and stable, rolling can make it behave unpredictably, resulting in tangles, broken yarn, or slipping yarn.

Exceptions to the generalization that rolling is more forceful include large supported spindles like Navajo or Nordic lap spindles, which you typically spin by rolling along the length of your thigh and drafting a length of yarn using the accumulated twist. You might also roll a large support spindle to spin with a one-handed drafting method.

exercise ROLLING

Attach a long leader to your spindle, preferably a plied yarn that will hold together well, so that at least a yard of leader comes off the spindle. (You will probably want to be sitting down.) Secure the leader to your spindle by threading it through a hook and/or notch or by using a half-hitch. Hold the leader 12–18"

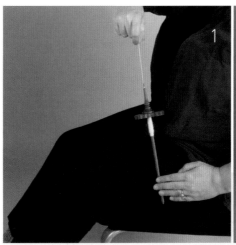

how to **roll the spindle**
1–2 Rolling a spindle between your palm and thigh sets it in motion quickly.

from the spindle with one hand and use the other hand to roll it down the thigh opposite the hand holding the leader. Try rolling it on the outside of the opposite thigh first. The spindle should fly out into the air, but not fall. Practice getting the hand that did the rolling up to the hand that's holding the leader and then moving both hands apart. Move your setting-in-motion hand up and down gently on the leader yarn, feeling for the twist moving. Watch as your leader gets very twisty! Feel for the twist in the leader starting to counteract the spindle's rotation. Switch hands and repeat this exercise. Keep going, alternating hands each time.

Next, try rolling down along the inside of the thigh on the same side of your body as the hand holding your leader. Lastly, try rolling up the outside of your thigh. Again, alternate which hand is doing what job. Each time, practice feeling the twist as it moves through your leader yarn with your forward hand.

If you roll down the outside of your left thigh, your spindle will spin clockwise, or Z. If you roll up outside of the left thigh, it will go counterclockwise, or S. Rolling down the outside of the right thigh is the opposite: you go S; and up the outside of the right thigh, Z. You may prefer to roll along the inside of your thigh, in which case the directions are reversed.

Ready to really shake it up? Practice the outside-of-the-thigh rolls while walking across the room. You will probably need to bring one leg up a little as if to step up a flight of stairs.

exercise ROLL BETWEEN YOUR FEET
You'll need enough shaft at the bottom of your spindle so that the cop or whorl clears the top of your foot when the spindle touches the ground and enough length of leader to hold on to while you have the spindle touching the ground; two yards should give you plenty of extra play.

Place the spindle bottom next to your left foot along the inside, a little forward of the instep, and put your right foot on the other side with toes even with your left foot. Pull your right foot back, rolling the spindle base along your left foot. This spins your spindle clockwise, or Z.

Walk some leader up on your hand so you can control the spindle's swing, then lower it again until it rests against the inside of your right foot. Repeat the exercise, this time pulling your left foot back. This spins the spindle in a counterclockwise, or S, direction.

getting hands in position

Whichever method you use, you will need to be able to quickly move your hands into position to draft. If you're spinning supported using one hand to keep the spindle in motion and one hand to draft, you're all set, but if you are using a two-handed drafting method, you'll need to move one or both hands. Your dominant hand will generally be able to move faster and get into drafting position more quickly.

When you start a suspended spindle, the hand you use will be your forward hand when drafting with a two-handed method. This hand will control your

how to **start the spindle with your feet**

1 Stand with the shaft of the spindle between your feet.

2 Pull your right foot back, rolling the spindle along your left arch.

twist; usually this means the hand with the superior fine motor control—your dominant hand. It's especially worth looking which hand you use to do what task at if you are flicking your spindle to get it started.

If you spin supported with a one-handed drafting method, it's also worth trying it both ways—swap which hand does the spindle-turning and which hand holds your fiber and drafts. You may be startled to find that what you first assumed isn't what's actually the most comfortable (and therefore fastest and most productive) for you.

Drafting Fibers and Spinning Yarn

How you draft has a tremendous impact on how your yarn turns out. If you draft with worsted methods, where twist only enters fibers held under tension after being fully attenuated, your yarn will be denser and smoother, without a lot of air trapped inside the fibers.

With a suspended spindle, most spinners find it easiest to spin with a worsted technique, drafting a short length of fiber, keeping twist out with the hand closest to the spindle, and sliding the twist into those drafted fibers. In this technique, the fibers do not bear the weight of the spindle while they are being drafted; that only happens once twist has entered and yarn is formed. You keep your fiber supply in one hand, while the other sets the spindle in motion, manages twist in your yarn, and drafts.

handedness

Many spinners hold their fiber supply in the nondominant hand, leaving the dominant hand with the more varied (and possibly more difficult) set of jobs to do. In some cultures, though, spinners switch hands depending on what direction the yarn is being spun. There are a lot of practical reasons to practice drafting with either hand, not least of which is to determine what really is the quickest for you.

sensing twist

Most spinners find that one hand has a greater ability to feel twist in motion than the other. You can view that as your dominant spinning hand, even if it isn't the hand you view as dominant for other tasks. This matters because a major factor in being very effective and fast at drafting with a spindle is being able to feel the twist moving.

Unlike a wheel, whose rate of twist generation doesn't change so long as you keep treadling at a steady rate, spindles do change speeds. Your ability to judge how that's happening and act on it is literally a make-or-break skill when spinning with a suspended spindle. If you can tell that the spindle is starting to slow down and soon you will not be generating new twist, you can stop the spindle and wind on your spun yarn

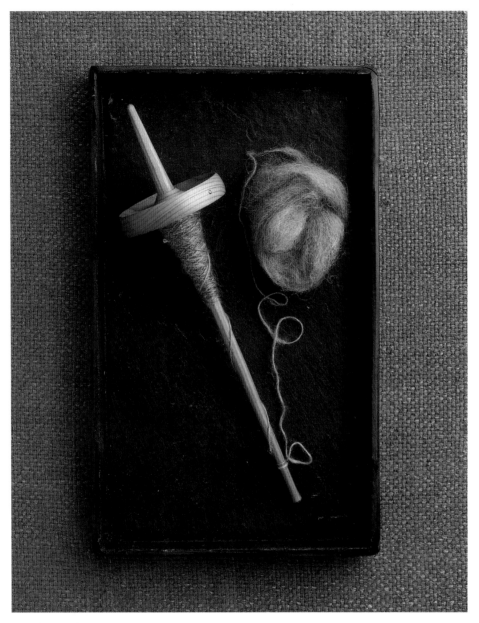

all the things to track, but after practice, you handle it all at a reflexive level like the many things you track while driving a car.

exercise FEEL FOR TWIST

With the hand that is closer to the spindle, try to feel the twist moving through the yarn. If that hand can't feel it, try switching hands. It may not feel right immediately, but keep an open mind—all you're checking for is whether or not you can feel the twist with your fingertips.

hand positioning

Spinning on a spindle gives your hands great freedom of position, which allows for a few drafting tricks that are rarely (if ever) possible on a wheel. For one thing, you can bring your other fingers into the mix. With thumb and forefinger pinching off the twist and pulling fiber out of your fiber supply, you're concentrating two jobs into just two fingertips the entire time you're drafting. But what if you used your thumb and middle finger to pinch off the twist and your index finger to pull yarn out of your fiber supply? What if you also used your ring finger and pinkie to feel for twist in your freshly spun yarn? If you can learn those things, you have a lot of options for fine-grained control of your yarn.

These tricks open up whole new worlds in production speed with spindles. Developing a feel for how much twist is in that yarn you've just spun

---

before the spindle starts to backspin and your fresh yarn falls apart.

If you are a seasoned spindle spinner, you probably do that without thinking about it. You may even take that further: instead of stopping and winding on when your spindle begins to slow down,

you may set it in motion again to spin a longer span of yarn before it's time to store it on your spindle. Your hands have probably developed an instinctive dance that includes many steps you no longer think about. When you first start out, it seems like you'll never get the hang of

makes you confident that it'll bear the weight of a spindle. If your pinkie detects there isn't quite enough, there's time for you to get more in before your yarn drifts apart. If your ring finger detects a little slub, you have a chance to correct it.

drafting methods

Using four fingers plus a thumb to control the drafting process, you have access to drafting methods that aren't purely worsted. You can let a controlled amount of twist into your drafting zone—and the fiber in your drafting zone doesn't have to hold the weight of the spindle yet. This permits a woolen draw, as well as double-drafting, even when spinning suspended. Long draw, a woolen technique, is at the opposite end of the spectrum from the worsted techniques discussed so far. Where worsted technique requires that your fibers be fully drafted before adding twist, woolen techniques need twist in the drafting zone in order to work. In woolen spinning, the twist plays an active role in the drafting of your fibers.

Woolen methods are often faster per yard than worsted methods, meaning they're well-suited to producing a lot of yarn quickly. They also enable a variety of other techniques. For example, spinners in the Andes produce astonishing quantities of fine, durable weaving yarn extremely quickly by double-drafting, in which the second pass is done with worsted techniques.

length before wind-on

How long a span of yarn you can spin between wind-ons is also a big factor in production rate, as is your comfort level in executing the movements in the entire process. Extended time with your hands raised higher than your shoulders will grow uncomfortable quickly, so it's impractical to spin a greater length of yarn just by reaching up over your head. What's more, the longer your spun yarn is, the more your spindle will sway and the harder it may be to control.

Spinners have solved this by understanding that although twist prefers to move in a straight line, it will travel around a corner if you make it. The length of yarn you're spinning isn't limited to just the distance between your hands and the ground; you can add the distance between your two hands to keep drafting and adding twist between wind-ons. In order to move twist this way, you need to use your forward hand, sliding it back and forth a bit on your spun yarn. Once you're comfortable with this, you can completely change the angle at which you are drafting—instead of spinning with a vertical drafting zone (which comes naturally to many spinners), you can spin horizontally. This is more comfortable for the long haul and lets you spin a length of yarn longer than you are tall, or longer than your armspan.

The tricky part is that you have to keep your freshly spun singles under tension while getting ready to wind on. If you lose tension on it, it will be very prone to tangling. So how do you keep it under tension? A clever solution is to give your fiber supply hand one more job to do: walk your yarn up onto any two fingers of your fiber supply hand as if to make a butterfly.

Being able to store your spun yarn on your fingers like this is also closely related to getting the most out of double-drafting. First, it lets you handle a much greater length of yarn; and second, you will often need to store your first-pass drafted fibers on your fingers in while making the fine-tuning second pass.

exercise SPIN WITHOUT WINDING ON

Sit or stand on something high off the ground (at the edge of a balcony or a retaining wall, for example). Expect to drop your spindle—don't do this with one that is fragile or that you're unwilling to drop! You may want to put a pillow or rug underneath where your spindle will be hanging. Set your spindle in motion over the edge and start drafting. When you can feel it begin to lose spin, walk the spun yarn up on your fiber supply hand, and set the spindle in motion again. Feed out the temporarily stored yarn, letting it take on more twist, until it's all fed out and you can start to draft new yarn. Keep going until you reach the ground.

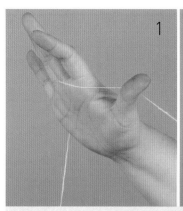 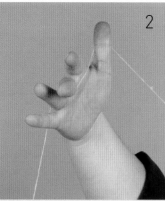 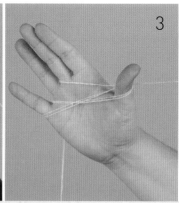 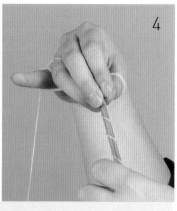

how to **wind a butterfly**

1 Wind the yarn around your fiber-control hand so that it travels behind your pinkie and ring finger, in front of your middle and index fingers, and behind your thumb.

2 Turn your hand so your palm faces you and catch the yarn that leads to the spindle with your pinkie, so that it crosses your palm again.

3 Turn your hand palm forward again and catch the yarn that leads to the spindle with your thumb. You'll have a cross in the palm of your hand now. Repeat until the spindle is in easy reach.

4 Slip the half-hitch off the shaft and unwind the yarn spiraled up the shaft. You're all set to wind on, feeding off the butterfly stored on your fingers.

exercise WIND A BUTTERFLY

Storing your spun yarn on your hand, crossing your palm between thumb and pinkie fingers, allows you to keep your freshly spun yarns under tension so you can work with a great length of yarn without having to stretch and strain. It allows you to control yarn longer than your armspan or your height, work in close quarters, and avoid a lot of fatigue in the arms and shoulders.

exercise TEAM SPINNING

Play this game with a friend. One of you sets the spindle in motion and keeps it in motion while the other drafts. See how far apart from each other you can get. Take turns. If you can keep generating twist, it'll keep moving through any length of yarn. How far can you push it? Let each other know when you can feel the twist stopping. Is it at the same time as the spindle is slowing?

Winding On

When you timed yourself on the four basic steps, you may have been surprised to discover how much time you spent winding yarn onto your spindle. Many spinners spend the same amount of time winding on as spinning that length of yarn!

However, if you time yourself at the beginning of a spindle full of yarn, and then again at the end, you will find it takes less time at the end. The circumference of the fuller spindle is greater, and each wrap around the spindle takes up more yarn. You can wind the same length of yarn onto the spindle in fewer wraps, and fewer wraps translates to less time spent winding on.

One easy way to reduce the number of wraps needed to get your yarn onto the spindle is by winding at an angle, in sort of an X configuration. This method has a number of advantages, not least of them that it tends to make your cops much sturdier and less prone to slipping around. This is particularly appealing if you are spinning with a low-whorl spindle whose shaft is a little slippery or with fibers that are.

Most veteran spindle spinners will use a variety of methods in concert. Each individual spindle will require some time to determine what works best for that spindle and the spinner using it.

cop location

Another thing to consider is the placement of the cop. While modern spinners often instinctively place cops right up against spindle whorls, old paintings, carvings, and other depictions clearly show some ancient spinners winding cops at a distance from the whorl.

Cops wound close to the whorl seem to be most common in cultures that used top whorls and seem to have primarily set their spindles in motion with a roll rather than a flick. Placing a cop away from the whorl seems to have been most common in cultures with low-whorl spindles or where spindles didn't necessarily have a whorl. In these cases the cops are often concentrated close to the center of the spindle's length, spreading out toward both ends with a bulbous growth outward in the center.

cop weight

The fuller a spindle is, the faster a spinner tends to produce yardage of spun yarn, right up to the point that the stored yarn poses an obstacle to spinning. When that point arrives is individual; most production spindle spinners try to push that as far as they can, knowing that the more they spin, the faster it goes. But being able to push these boundaries comes by feel and practice, and it varies from spindle to spindle and fiber to fiber.

In this respect, the choices available to modern spinners could hinder our production rates: where a pre-industrial spinner might have had only one type of spindle for an entire lifetime, contemporary spinners can be exposed to a wide range. We develop generalist skills rather than deep expertise with one specific tool.

exercise WIND A COP

Take a skein of yarn of a size you'd like to fit on a spindle and wind a cop. You can wind on without securing the yarn as if to spin, or you can do it a length at a time. Do you find it makes a difference in what the wind-on feels like? Does your hand get tired? If you feel your hand tiring, push it for a count of ten past that, then stop and take a break for at least 90 seconds. You might not think so, but this builds quite a bit of strength. It lets you think about your cop shape and placement with no distractions and really get a feel for how much yarn you can pack on a spindle.

Securing Your Yarn

Securing spun yarn to the spindle so it doesn't just come right off when you continue spinning is another surprising time sink. Even with a spindle with a hook or notch, you can spend a lot of time getting this accomplished—and it'll be different from spindle to spindle. What works with one type of hook doesn't necessarily work well with another.

The big secret is shockingly simple: the technique that will be the fastest is whatever you can do without looking. Surprisingly, this is also usually the most secure.

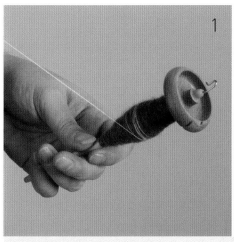

how to **wind a cop**

1   One method for winding a cop is simply to wind around the same place, making concentric circles on the shaft.

2   By winding up and down the shaft in an X, you can wind the yarn on faster.

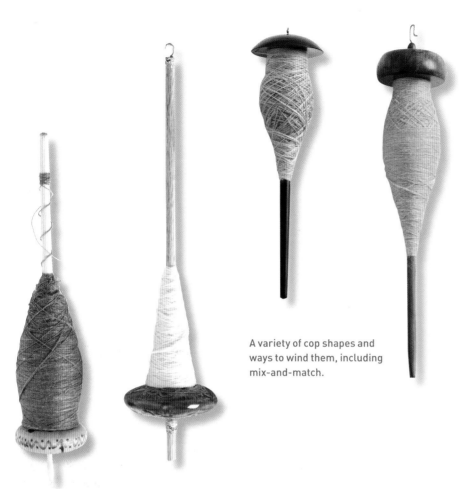

A variety of cop shapes and ways to wind them, including mix-and-match.

How you choose to secure your yarn can affect what methods you use to set it in motion. If you wind yarn under the whorl on a low whorl and then straight up to the top of the shaft, you'll have a length of yarn off to the side that precludes setting the spindle in motion by rolling. However, this type of wind-on makes it easy to release the half-hitch from a spindle with a shaft that has a notch or an outward flare at the top. With a Turkish spindle that has a knob at the top of the shaft, guiding the yarn straight from the cop to the half-hitch (see page 56) may be an advantage. But if rolling the spindle to set it in motion is important to you, you'll prefer spiraling up the shaft. Decide which low-whorl wind-on to use based on your preferences and the design of each spindle.

leader length

As your cop grows larger, you may find it harder to leave yourself the exact length of leader you want. One quick way to deal with that is by flicking your spindle to set it in motion, catching it in your hand, and quickly drafting out just enough yarn to make a longer leader. This tends to be more efficient than rewinding and re-securing your yarn to get a different length of leader. Since you need a longer leader to use a rolling method of setting the spindle in motion, you may find it advantageous to be able to spin more leader in this semi-supported way, by flicking the spindle and catching it—sort of like parking and drafting, but quicker than many park-

create a STOP

If your top-whorl spindle doesn't have a notch in the whorl, you can create a "stop" to help keep the yarn from slipping around. Leave a longer leader than usual and bring the yarn from under the whorl to over it behind the hook, through the hook, back under the whorl and around the shaft, then back up and through the hook. The stop should help keep the leader in place.

and-draft methods. It's also useful when you're spinning short-stapled fibers in suspended mode: you can make a longer leader in a semi-supported manner by flicking.

exercise FLICKING AND CATCHING

Practice setting the spindle with a short leader, catching it, and drafting out more fibers for a longer leader. Develop a sense for what amount of twist will be enough to hold the fibers together without making it difficult to draft out farther. This technique works with woolen and worsted drafting methods.

exercise SECURE YOUR YARN

Practice just securing your yarn to the spindle so you can keep spinning. Whether you use a half-hitch, wraparound a hook, or another method, practice securing and unsecuring your yarn. Once you feel reasonably quick at it, switch hands.

exercise ALL OF THE ABOVE—BLIND

You might be surprised what happens when you close your eyes. Things you think you have down to a reflex may be using more conscious and visual faculties than you think. Some of the finest and fastest spinners in the world are blind. This is because the hand truly can be quicker than the eye. Closing your eyes or blindfolding yourself to spin for a little while can be incredibly enlightening. It will really develop your physical sense of the yarn you're spinning, the tools you're working with, and what your body does.

how to **flick and catch**

1 With a relatively short leader, flick the spindle to start.

2 Quickly move your flicking hand into position to catch the spindle when enough twist has been generated, then draft out additional fibers for a longer leader portion.

exercise ALL OF THE ABOVE—PLUS SOMETHING ELSE

To really find out whether an action is reflexive and reinforce it, try doing it while singing a song or reciting a poem (or even reading one)—something it takes a little brainpower to do. Distract your mind from what your hands are doing. Can they keep going without your telling them what to do? Do this once every week or two as a pop quiz. Do you default to any particular way of performing tasks once your mind is on something else?

Some of these exercises are aimed at finding your bottlenecks so you can work through them from a logical perspective: looking at the mechanics of what you're doing and trying different ways to improve your efficiency and thus your speed. Others are all about the body mechanics. Bear in mind that your personal ergonomics will differ from anyone else's—and this is one of the major advantages spindles offer. Maximizing your personal productivity will require you to look at both the brain stuff and the body stuff and devote time to practicing the body stuff.

Make notes about your production rate the first time you measure it, then put that aside for a month while working with these exercises. After that month, measure again and take stock of what's changed. Then you can revisit the exercises and continue fine-tuning your own personal productivity.

WHICH SPINDLE WHEN

It's common for spinners at various levels of expertise to ask what spindle should be used for what specific task, and I'd love to be able to give you a simple, straightforward answer. The truth, however, is that there is no easy answer. Every spinner is different, every project is different, and throughout history all over the world, spinners have used a wide range of tools to do the same basic jobs. There are no absolute rules about what spindle you must use for what purpose, although there are amazing techniques from the living spindle traditions of the world that can enrich any spinner's experience. There is always something to be learned from studying a new yarn-making tool, and sadly, there are far more than we could ever fit into one single book. We've selected a few types of specialty spindle to investigate in a little more depth.

Supported Spindles

Small supported spindles are the tool of choice for many cultures working primarily with very fine, short-stapled fibers. When you're spinning with a small supported spindle, the base rests either in a bowl or on another surface, which bears the weight of the spindle. This support reduces the tensile strain on the yarn, so you don't have to worry about spinning the yarn fast enough to bear the weight of the spindle. That changes the relationship between the kind of yarn you can spin and the weight and shape of the spindle.

A large support spindle used in your lap, like a Navajo or Nordic lap spindle, is typically intended to spin a thick yarn. It can be difficult to spin such a thick yarn on a suspended spindle because you'd need a very heavy spindle to overcome the stored twist energy in a thick yarn. A spindle small enough to be used suspended will have more limited capacity to store very thick yarn than a larger one that doesn't have to be used suspended.

Tahkli

A tahkli is commonly found in Asia, the Middle East, and North Africa. Tahklis often look like small low-whorl suspended spindles with very slender shafts and pointed bottom tips. The tahkli shown here spinning some cotton sliver has no hook on the shaft, though some do. When spinning on a tahkli, I use a bowl if I'm spinning in my lap, if the tahkli wants to go skidding around on a table, or if I want to protect a surface's finish from possible small scratches from the tahkli's sharp point.

Because a tahkli is heavy for its size, center-weighted, and has a very narrow shaft with a sharp tip at the base to reduce friction, it is capable of tremendous speed and sustained spin. This makes it terrific for spinning cotton or other short-stapled fibers, which require a fair amount of fast-moving twist to become stable yarn. Since it's supported, the yarn being formed does not need to bear the weight of the spindle at any time, so you can spin lofty, lower-twist yarns with a tahkli as well. Since it is very small, however, it's not suited to spinning thick yarn. Use a tahkli to spin fine yarn from short-stapled fibers or fine yarn with a low twist or a lot of loft from any fibers.

If your tahkli has a hook, you can quickly spin yourself a leader, starting by catching the unspun fiber in the hook. If you don't have a hook, you may prefer to use a pre-spun leader. You will need enough yarn to wrap around the bottom near the whorl a few times, then spiral

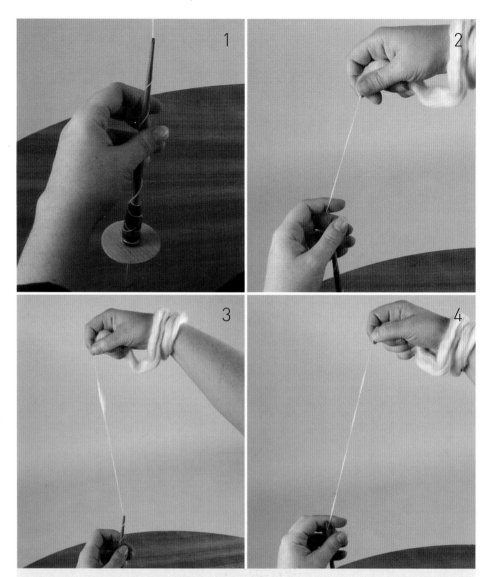

how to **spin on a tahkli**

1 Spin or attach enough yarn to wind several times around the shaft near the whorl, then spiral the yarn up the shaft.

2 Set the spindle in motion and build up a lot of twist in the leader portion.

3 With the spindle still in motion, draw back your fiber hand in one motion, keeping the spindle in motion with the other hand if necessary.

4 Pinch off the twist and pull back farther, letting the slubs thin out.

up the shaft to the hook and leave several inches beyond that.

spin cotton on a tahkli

Rest the tahkli on a table surface or in a bowl. With a finger-flick, set the tahkli in motion. Store up lots of twist in your leader portion—and I do mean lots! You will need it to turn short-stapled cotton into yarn quickly.

Once you have a lot of twist in your leader portion, draft back with one quick motion of your fiber-supply hand. Your other hand is ready to keep the tahkli in motion. This is a one-handed long draw method, classified as a woolen technique.

With the tahkli still in motion, use your fiber-supply hand to pinch the end of your just-spun yarn closest to the fiber supply. Gently tug back farther and watch any slubs from your initial draw start to disappear.

When you have as long a length of yarn as you can manage, you can use your spindle-controlling hand to go over the length you've just spun, compressing any slubs and checking for irregularities in twist.

Unwind the yarn that spirals up the shaft. Store this on your fingers in a butterfly if necessary. Wind on the new length of spun yarn close to the tahkli's whorl spiral a length up the shaft and through the hook again (if applicable).

Tibetan or Russian Spindle

Tibetan and Russian spindles are among the last examples of this spindle form still be found in regular use. Spinners in Tibet use them to make yarn from cashmere and yak downs, and lace knitters in and around Russia use them to produce very fine singles from down fibers, such as the down of Orenburg goats (more similar to cashmere than mohair).

The major difference between Russian and Tibetan variants of this spindle form is that Tibetan spindles feature a whorl, while Russian examples do not. In this case, the whorl's major purpose is to aid with cop formation—it doesn't have a major impact on how the spindle performs, but it allows a spinner to build a much larger cop with greater ease. Russian spinners still put quite a bit of yarn on their spindles, but the skill to do so stably is one it takes time to build. Another key difference is that due to size, mass distribution, and shape, this spindle form tends to spin more slowly than tiny support spindles like a tahkli, making it more suited to lower-twist and potentially thicker yarns. (In the photos below, I'm using techniques from the Russian tradition with the Tibetan spindle; there's no reason not to mix and match as desired.)

In the Orenburg tradition, these singles are held together with an industrially produced fine silk yarn and wound doubled onto another spindle. This double-stranded yarn is then plied with a very light plying twist, so little that most contemporary spinners would judge it extremely underplied.

While gossamer-fine and seemingly fragile, yarns produced in this manner are actually very durable. Traditional Orenburg lace shawls are knitted from this yarn, which in the skein looks limp and delicate. Once knitted up and worn for a while, the shawls take on an incredible halo and are not only beautiful but warm.

You will want a smooth-drafting, nicely prepared fiber for this. Compacted or stiff-drafting fibers usually won't be a good choice, but a fluffy cloud of down fibers works great.

spin russian-style

Rest the spindle in a bowl. Attach a leader and spiral it up the shaft to the point, making the spirals tighter closer to the point. Holding your fiber in one hand and the spindle in the other, set the spindle in motion. Make a circle with thumb and forefinger, keeping those fingers hovering around the tip of your spindle. Build up twist in your leader where it comes off the tip.

Keep an eye on the spindle's motion—don't let it stop or backspin! If it does, the yarn will come right off the spindle. There's nothing securing the yarn to the spindle, so you have to do that with your hands. With twist built up in your leader, attach the new fiber. Keep the spindle in motion by twirling again with small motions and draft back with your fiber-supply hand away from the spindle at a slight angle.

Once your fiber is fully drafted to your desired thickness, you may wish to add a little more twist to it if it seems slippery

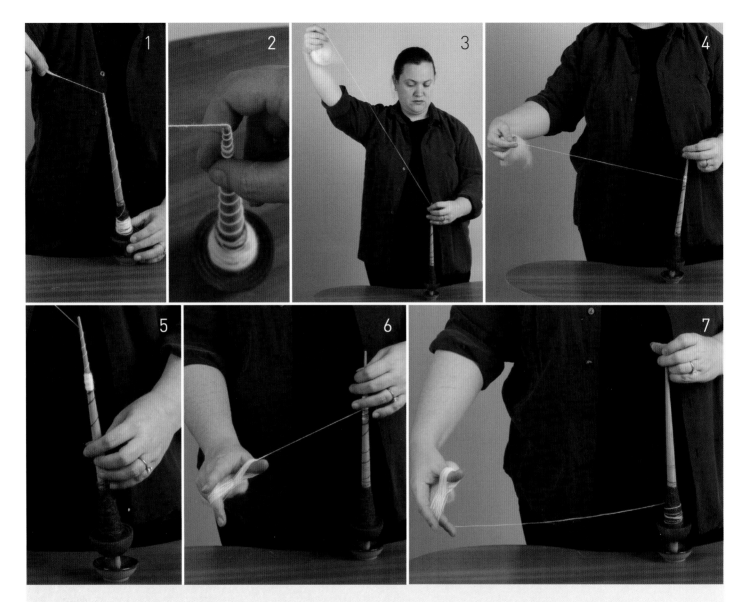

how to **spin russian-style**

1 Rest the spindle in a bowl. Attach the leader and spiral it up the shaft, with the spirals tighter near the tip than the base.

2 Set the spindle in motion, keeping the thumb and forefingers of your spindle hand in a circle around the tip.

3 Draw back with your fiber hand at a slight angle to the spindle and draft out a length of fiber.

4 Wind the new yarn in a temporary cop near the tip of the spindle.

5 Wind the yarn up from the temporary cop in tight spirals to the tip.

6 When the temporary cop becomes unwieldy, unwind the yarn onto your fingers.

7 Wind the yarn onto the permanent cop at the base of the spindle.

This Russian-style spindle is intended for supported use and has been decorated with colorful lines.

and not cohesive; just hold the length out and spin the spindle a little longer. Unwind a little bit and wind the whole leader down toward the base, leaving enough to begin the process again. Spiral the new yarn up the spindle (in tighter circles near the tip). Spin another length of fiber, but this time store your new length of yarn closer to the tip of the spindle (but not at the tip precisely). Make a few tight spirals close to the top and spin another length.

You can store several spun lengths at a time near the tip in a temporary cop. Once that gets cumbersome, unwind it by storing it on your fingers in a butterfly, then wind a more permanent cop down toward the base of the spindle. This saves time winding on and allows you to focus on the stability of your cop—something that can be very important with extremely fine, soft, fuzzy yarn.

Navajo Spindle

A Navajo-style large support spindle is an excellent choice for spinning thick, low-twist yarns. You can use it while it's turning, by drafting with one hand, or in a park-and-draft method with a two-handed draw. These spindles are a great way to spin a larger volume of thick yarn, because their size allows you to store a great deal of yarn, which you wouldn't be able to do on a spindle of a size it would be possible to spin suspended. The Navajo people use these spindles to produce thick rug and blanket yarn and cordage for a variety of purposes. (See step-by-step photographs on page 96.)

spin navajo-style

To use a Navajo spindle, spin a leader using the same method as for spinning off a stick (see page 52). Spiral the leader up the shaft. With the leader coming off the tip, lay the spindle across your thigh at an angle to your leg. Gently roll it on your thigh to generate twist.

Using your fiber-supply hand, draft back while you roll the spindle with the other hand. It won't take much work: let lots of fiber out as you go and allow the slow-moving twist to take it.

Unwind the yarn that spirals up the spindle shaft and rewind it around the base near the whorl. Wind on your spun yarn and spiral the last part of it up the shaft.

Specialty Suspended and Hybrid Spindles

Different cultures have evolved an astonishing array of spindles that are primarily used suspended as well as spindles that may be used in multiple modes (suspended, supported, or switching back and forth). Suspended-spindle use is appealing if you like to spin while walking around, and it's also popular with spinners of longer-stapled fibers (which stabilize as yarn quickly and easily). It's also possible to spin a longer length in between wind-ons if you are spinning suspended. On the other hand, delicate or short fibers may be tricky to spin suspended at first—though there are absolutely spinners who do so without issue.

A spindle intended for suspended use commonly (but not always) features a ready means of anchoring yarn to the spindle (such as a hook or notch). There is also often a more pronounced difference between shaft and whorl than is seen on some spindles intended for supported use (like the Russian one above or French one on page 16).

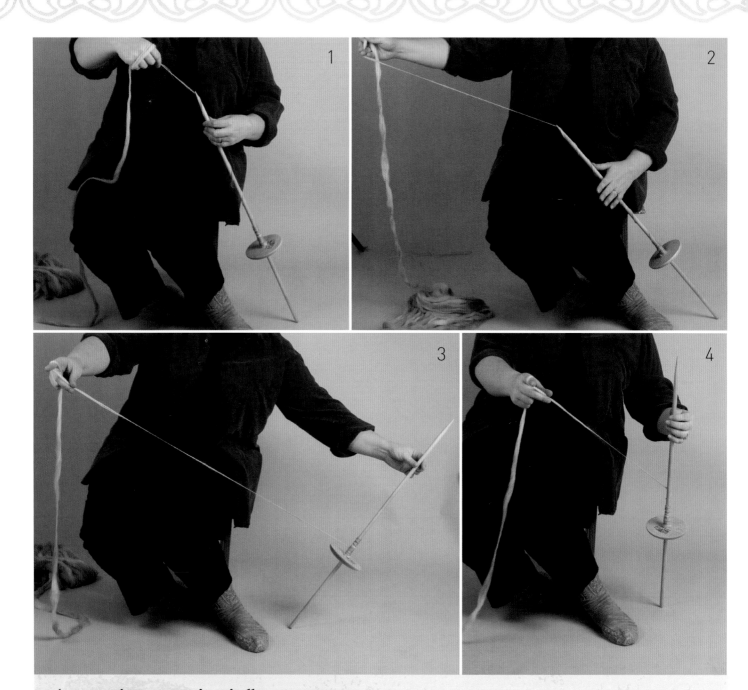

how to **spin on a navajo spindle**

1 Spin a leader and spiral it up to the tip of the spindle.

2 Roll the spindle on your thigh to generate twist and begin to draft out fiber. Draft out a long length of fiber and allow the slow-moving twist to move into it.

3 Hold the spindle away from you, unwind the yarn that spirals up the shaft, and rewind it near the whorl.

4 Leave enough yarn to serve as a leader and spiral it up the shaft to begin spinning again.

Turkish Spindle

A Turkish spindle spins essentially like any other low-whorl spindle, differing mainly in that its crossbar structure allows you to wind your cop differently than simply storing it around the spindle's shaft. Some Turkish spindles also have a distinctive knob at the top of the shaft, which accommodates a slightly different technique to secure the yarn to the shaft.

a diferent kind of cop

Wind your spun yarn under one arm, and across to the opposite arm, wrap under, and across several times. It may help to think, "Over two, under one."

When your Turkish spindle is full, you can slide the entire mass of crossbars and cop up the shaft and remove it. Once off the shaft, the crossbars can be slid out one at a time, and you're left with a center-pull ball, ready to use or ply from.

securing yarn

If your spindle's shaft has a bit of a knob at the top, you may want to secure your yarn differently than on other suspended spindles. When you've wound yarn onto the cop and are ready to spin again, bring the leader portion straight up to the top of the shaft and make a half-hitch (see page 56). On a spindle with a knobbed shaft such as some Turkish spindles feature, this is quick and easy to release—just put your thumb under

When the arms of a Turkish spindle are removed, the cop forms a center-pull ball.

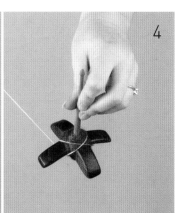

how to **wind a cop on a turkish spindle**

1 The crossed arms of a Turkish spindle interlock for easy storage and removal of the spun yarn.

2 Wrap the yarn over two arms and under one.

3 Wrap over two to the opposite arm.

4 This method wraps the yarn evenly around the arms.

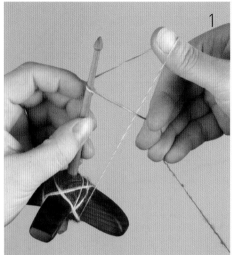

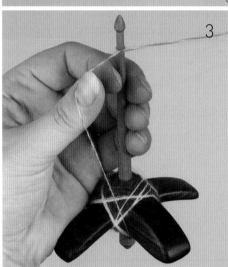

how to **secure yarn to a turkish spindle with knobbed shaft**

1 Make a half-hitch just below the knob.

2 Pull it snug to spin.

3 To remove the half-hitch, slip your thumb beneath the yarn between the cop and half-hitch.

4 Use your thumb to loosen the half-hitch and remove it from the spindle.

the yarn and flick it off. Since your cop is well-stabilized by being wrapped around the spindle's arms down below, there's little risk of your spun yarn coming off. The big potential down side is that you're stuck with finger-flicking only if you've got that length of yarn that isn't staying close to the shaft. Having yarn not securely wrapped around the shaft but loose in the air makes rolling the spindle prohibitive. Yarn flying loose in the air can also destabilize the spindle's rotation, add drag, and cause you to lose spin sooner.

Akha Spindles

The Akha people of China, Laos, Myanmar, Vietnam, and Thailand are known for their artistry in many fields, and textiles are a major one. Living mostly as subsistence farmers, they are known for their exceptional cotton textiles.

Using mid-whorl spindles with a combination of techniques, Akha spinners produce fine cotton yarn that is used in weaving as both warp and weft and in embroidery. Traditional akha spindles are often made of metal, such as silver, by their master tribal metalworkers.

spin semi-supported

The Akha-style mid-whorl spindle is well-suited for hybrid use and has been seen in traditional communities being used first to draw out a length of yarn while supported in the hand, then to add more twist and make further yarn using a second, suspended draw. This method can be fantastic combined with double-drafting techniques.

With a mid-whorl spindle, the whorl is positioned centrally along the shaft, a placement some spinners contend is truly the ideal, as it most closely resembles the overall way in which weight ultimately becomes distributed as you wind more and more yarn onto the spindle. Some mid-whorl spinners cover the whorl entirely and wind two-part cops, above and below the whorl, which serves only as a weight to get things started initially.

And One More Thing . . .

Even considering the techniques associated with the cultural and historical origins of specialty spindles, there are still no spinning police who'll come and haul you off to yarn prison if you revise a technique or use a tool in your own way. Indeed, this is one of the major strengths of spindles over other spinning devices: they're flexible. It's like the difference between going to the gym and using the carefully designed exercise machines or using free weights. On one hand, the machines will more readily guarantee correctness of form and force you to do the exercise the most effective way. But if you can get comfortable with free weights, you can find infinite variation for your exercise routines. So it is with spindles. Do you like spinning supported, but don't like any of the spindles commonly sold as support

spin on an **akha spindle**

1 Twirl the spindle in one hand while drafting across the body with the other.

2 With an additional flick or a thigh roll, set the spindle in motion quickly and release it.

3 Draft out additionally while spinning suspended.

spindles—in fact, you really like high whorls? Go ahead and try your high-whorl drop spindle as a support spindle. If you like it, nothing says you can't use it that way. Do you like spinning cotton but not supported spindles? Give it a try on a suspended one. If it works for you, then it isn't wrong.

PLYING

Plying means taking spun singles and putting two or more of them together while adding twist in the opposite direction from which you first spun them. This sounds pretty simple, but it's possible to get into very complex structures with plying if you desire. There are lots of interesting effects possible with plying that can create an entirely different yarn from the singles.

Should you ply your yarn? That's up to you. Plying isn't an absolute requirement, but there are many benefits to plying your yarn, and lots of interesting things you can do with plying to create an entirely different yarn.

Plying adds a significant amount of strength to a yarn. When you spin, the twist adds strength to the fibers; plying adds even more. A two-ply yarn isn't just two times stronger than a singles yarn—the counteracting twist makes it exponentially stronger. Since the yarns are twisted together, fewer individual fibers are exposed to the wear and tear of the outside world, and more of the yarn's surface area is safely protected inside the yarn. Plied yarns are more resistant to wear and tear from friction or the elements, such as pilling, and also harder to break.

Another good reason to ply is to even out inconsistencies in your yarn. If your yarn is a little bit thick and thin, you will usually get a yarn that is less thick and thin when you ply it. Plying is one more step during which you can fine-tune your yarn into exactly what you want.

Plying can also allow unique design elements. You can create a variety of different effects with plied yarns that you can't do with singles. Different plying structures produce different kinds of fabric, and combining yarn structure with the technique and pattern of your choice gives you the ultimate control over your finished object.

In general, singles yarns will be more likely to create skew or bias in some fabrics, particularly knitting

A specially designed spindle kate holds spindles in place and helps keep yarn under tension for plying.

(though this effect is minimized by blocking or particular knitted stitches), and they will be most prone to stretch out of shape, wear thin, and pill. Plying minimizes these problems.

You may like your singles yarn just as it is, and there are lots of good uses for singles, even though they tend to be not as strong, not as consistent, and less structured than a plied yarn. It's important to understand how the decision to ply your yarn or not, and

your choice of plying structure, can affect your finished product made with your yarn.

Planning for Plying

Plying involves only two things (really!): yarn management and adding plying twist. That's it!

You can accomplish these two things in a seemingly limitless number of ways. When spinning with a wheel, it's common to work from bobbins full of singles. That's one of the advantages the bobbin-and-flyer wheel offers: as soon as you spin your yarn, it's packaged in a way that you can work with immediately. Just put the bobbins onto shafts where they can spin freely, take the yarn in hand, and ply onto another bobbin.

Plying from spindles may seem a little less straightforward. So how have spinners through the ages managed their yarn and added plying twist? Some cultures developed procedures to solve these problems, while others developed

tools. Contemporary spinners can mix and match these approaches to keep spun singles under control and serve them up to be plied in a way that is easy to handle, portable, and efficient.

Tools for Yarn Management

Many spinners try to treat spindles like bobbins: Spin one spindle full of singles, then another, and ply directly from them. The most obvious way to ply yarns spun on several spindles is to set them up so that you can wind yarn directly from them as you ply onto another spindle. There are some clever tools that make it easier to ply directly from spindles, like a spindle kate or an improvised shoebox kate. For spindles with hooks, hanging them from swiveling hooks may make it easier to ply from them. This approach isn't very portable, and it can be hard to combine yarn management and adding plying twist.

What if you only have one spindle? If you have a bobbin winder, you could

Place each ball of singles under a flowerpot with the yarn passing through the hole to keep the yarn from tangling as you wind a ball or ply.

use it to wind your spindle-spun singles onto bobbins, then ply from those back onto your spindle. But by that point, some would say that you might as well go ahead and ply the yarn on a wheel. Besides, you're already stuck in one place with your yarn management device close by, so you can't ply on the go.

One solution is to fill a spindle, wind that yarn into a ball, and set it aside for later. Fill the spindle again, wind that yarn into a ball, and ply from the two balls back onto your spindle. This works well enough, although balls don't generally unwind as neatly as bobbins do, and you may need to come up with a way to keep your balls of yarn from rolling around and tangling—for instance, by putting each ball underneath a small flowerpot and threading the yarn out

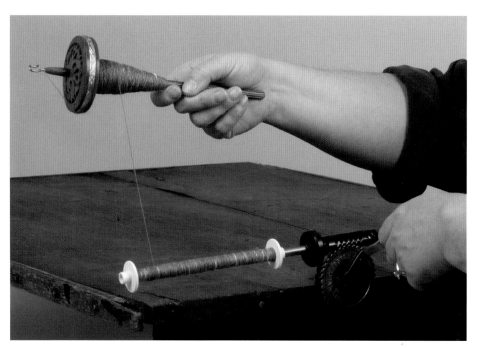

If you have a bobbin winder, you can use it to rewind a cop evenly from a spindle.

A shoebox with holes punched in the sides can hold spindles for plying.

through holes in the bottom of the pots. (You could simply slip the cop off the spindle and ply from that, but even the neatest cop isn't as neat as a ball wound all at once, leaving you vulnerable to tangling.)

Even if you aren't plying directly from these devices or using these tricks, they may make it easier for you to wind a multi-strand ball.

Plying from a Center-pull Ball

One solution to being tethered to your lazy kate (or upside-down flowerpots or what have you) is one that is also in common use by wheel spinners: Using a ball winder or nøstepinne (or your thumb!), wind a center-pull ball. Then hold the end that is coming off the outside together with the end coming from the inside together. Ply both ends all the way back to the middle with no leftover yarn. You can also carry that center-pull ball around with you. The downside to working from a center-pull ball is that as you feed yarn off both the inside and outside, the ball tends to lose structural integrity and becomes prone to tangling. This means you often have to stop plying for a little tangle management. Or possibly a lot of tangle management. It can be very frustrating.

wind a multi-strand ball

One good option is to wind your singles together into a multi-stranded yarn package. Andean spinners wind simultaneously from two spindles into a two-stranded skein, in which they then dye the yarn before plying—which

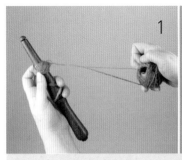

wind a **two-strand ball from one cop**

1 Wind a center-pull ball (shown here with a nøstepinne.

2 Hold the strands from the inside and outside of the ball together.

3 With the inner and outer strands under even tension, wind a new ball.

4 Don't worry if the strands twist around each other as long as they don't become tangled.

some do right from the skein, although it is more common to rewind it into a firm outer-feed ball that's easy to carry around and not prone to tangling. Russian spinners wind from two spindles onto a third, carrying the yarn together, then ply from that spindle full of doubled yarn onto another spindle.

This works well for any number of plies and has the benefit of separating your yarn management problems from introducing plying twist. It is especially approachable when paired with contemporary tools such as ball winders and bobbin winders.

Wind your full spindle off into a ball. You can wind this around a felt core, tennis ball, rubber ball—by any means with which you feel comfortable. Since singles coming off a spindle tend to get kinky, you may prefer to use an outer-feed ball instead of a center-pull ball. I

do, because this lets me store the yarn under tension, which eliminates the risk of tangles. Winding into a ball at this point also lets you find any problem spots in your singles and correct them on the spot, so I like to wind each cop of singles into an individual ball to be sure I don't have any surprises to manage.

Take the ends from both balls and hold them together. Wind these together into a two-stranded ball. While winding, take care to keep your singles from getting unevenly tensioned. You can do this with your hands alone (though you may find this takes practice to get the hang of) or by placing the balls in a bowl and

Did You Know?

The multi-strand yarn source idea isn't only for spindles—you can use it with a wheel, too. In fact, there are reports of it having been used routinely in European spinning communities where flyer wheels were prevalent, but most were equipped with only one bobbin. A lot of contemporary wheel-plying methods require you to keep individual plies separate right up to the moment when they're twisted together, but this really isn't necessary. Although you can do that with a spindle, it generally does not provide any benefit; in fact, it costs time and is less efficient and portable.

how to **wind a multi-strand ball from several spindles**

1 Secure several spindles (or cops) so that the yarn will unwind evenly without tangling.

2 Holding the individual strands under equal tension, wind a new ball with all the strands together.

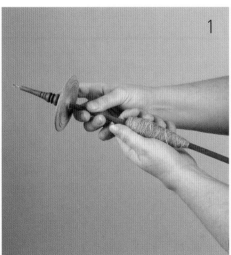

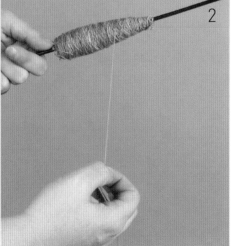

how to **slip a cop off a spindle**

1 A stable cop can be slipped down the shaft and onto a drinking straw of smaller diameter for easy removal.

2 Slipping a cop onto a knitting needle can make it easier to store or rewind.

letting them roll around while you wind. The "upstream" yarns may twist around each other; this isn't a problem unless they become outright tangled. Just keep an eye out for tangles starting to form, and if necessary, stop and solve them. Sometimes I wind two-stranded bobbins with my bobbin winder, especially with very fine yarn that will take a long time to wind by hand or a slippery one that would collapse and tangle easily in a center-pull ball.

You can also make a two-stranded ball by winding a center-pull ball, then winding the inside and outside strands together into another ball (center-pull or outer-pull, your choice). At first blush, this sounds like a lot of extra winding, but it saves time on yarn management while you are plying and makes your project entirely portable.

See the two strands together coming off that ball? Congratulations! You have completed the main yarn management portion of this exercise. Using this method, you can take your plying anywhere with you with only one spindle and work from yarn that's totally under control. While rewinding the yarn, you will also discover places in the singles that may need repairs. By rewinding, you also allow the twist in the yarn to distribute itself all the way through, creating greater consistency in that respect, as well.

This isn't just for two-ply yarns; you can wind any number of strands together. Imagine winding a center-pull ball, then winding it again into a double-stranded center-pull ball, then winding that ball doubled again. You'd have a four-ply ball ready to go!

If your cop is well-formed and stable, you may be able to slip it right off the spindle and work directly from it or slip it onto a temporary storage tool such as a drinking straw or knitting needle. Some spinners like to wrap a piece of paper tightly around the spindle shaft before beginning to spin so that the cop can be slipped off easily and so the tightly wound paper can serve as a core for the cop, preventing it from collapsing and tangling. Other spinners find the paper core to be too slippery, potentially even compromising the stability of the cop while spinning. It's your choice.

The Butterfly Method

Chances are you have used a variation on this technique to wind little pull-skeins of yarn or store leftover odds and ends, but didn't realize it had other uses, too. Use the same method to store yarn on your fingers as when you "walked" the yarn up onto your hand (see page 86) to store the entire length of yarn you want to ply. Hold both ends of the yarn together and attach them to the spindle. Gently remove the butterfly from your fingers, holding it at the cross in the figure eight to maintain the shape. As you add ply twist with the spindle, gently feed out yarn from both ends, maintaining even tension.

Plying from both ends and using crossed yarns to feed out smoothly is similar to the technique that has come to be known as "Andean plying," but this simpler method is much more commonly used in the Andes.

Plying Your Yarn

Attach your two-stranded ball to the spindle. Turning the spindle in the opposite direction from that which you used when you spun the singles, twist those strands together. Simply feed off that ball of yarn as you ply. When you have as much twisted yarn as you can manage, wind onto the spindle.

How Much Plying Twist?

This, too, is up to you. Spinners plying on wheels are commonly advised to count the number of treadles in a certain length of yarn fed out and use that number to determine how many twists are in each inch of their yarn (and to keep the plying twist consistent throughout), but you obviously can't do that with a spindle—there's no good way to count its rotations, and trying would be a nightmare. The bottom line (and this is true for wheel plying as well as spindle plying) is that you have to look at your yarn, feel it, and make a judgment call. You'll need to learn to tell this by eyeball and by touch. A good way see the amount of twist and learn if you're plying evenly is by plying together two singles in contrasting colors. This will allow you to really see what your plying twist looks like from one length of yarn to the next.

In the long run, becoming comfortable with making these judgments will likely lead to greater speed and comfort when plying with a wheel as well. As you get better at seeing the plying twist, you'll also train your hands to feel it, and soon all plying will become something you can do without thinking or even looking.

Basic Plying

Plying tends to go much more quickly than spinning, which means most suspended spinners prefer to set their spindle in motion with a roll to ply, as this is faster than a finger-flick. Here's a typical plying sequence using a high-whorl spindle and a double-stranded plying ball (see page 103). This works just as well with a non-portable yarn source, such as a spindle kate, balls under a flowerpot, or storage bobbins.

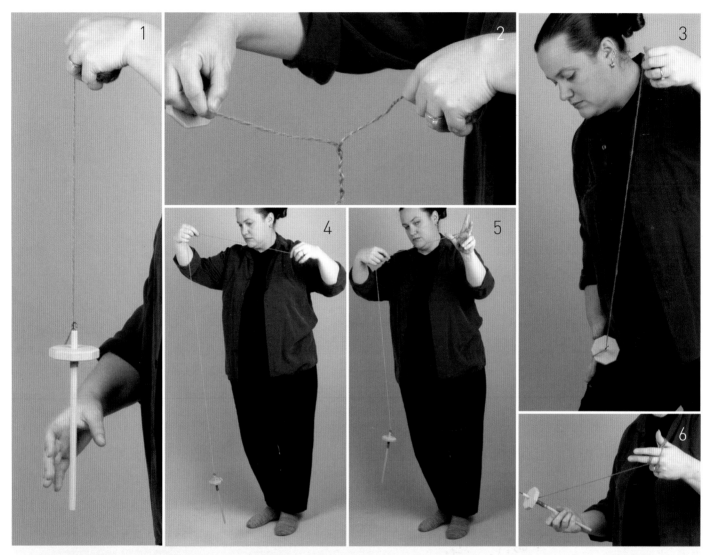

how to **ply**

1. Hold your double-stranded ball in one hand and attach the doubled yarns to be plied to your spindle.

2. Your yarn will probably attempt to self-ply slightly, but it needs more plying twist than that in order to become a stable yarn.

3. Set your spindle in motion in the opposite direction from that in which you originally spun your singles, in this case with a thigh roll.

4. Carefully feed yarn off your double-stranded ball, allowing it to become twisted by the spindle's motion. Keep the twist from getting all the way up into your ball.

5. Keep the freshly plied yarn under tension so it does not tangle. You can control a large length of yarn by walking it up your fingers in a butterfly (see page 86).

6. Wind the freshly plied yarn onto your spindle, gradually feeding yarn out from the butterfly so it stays under tension at all times. Secure your yarn to the spindle and repeat this sequence.

Plying in the Andean Manner

In the Andes, low-whorl spindles are set in motion for plying by rolling the spindle's shaft between the hands and releasing the spindle into the air. Although this method could be used when spinning, there's greater risk of yarn breakage with singles, and you need to use so much leader that it doesn't allow for a lot of new yarn to be spun before you must wind on. Therefore, this means of spin initiation is not typically used for spinning, but instead, only for plying.

This method depends on a hookless, notchless low-whorl spindle with a fairly smooth shaft, to which yarn is secured by spiraling it up the shaft and finishing with a half-hitch. Anything else is likely to either snag the yarn or cause the spinner hand pain. It also requires familiarity with the butterfly method of walking yarn up on your fingers to keep it under tension. You can use either hand, but one hand will be your yarn control hand and the other your spindle hand.

Just as rolling the spindle down the thigh sets it in motion faster than a finger-flick can, so does rolling it between your hands. You can build up very impressive speed this way, and it's a comfortable, easy way to roll the spindle while you are walking, which can't be said of rolling along your thigh. This is a very fast, efficient means of plying a lot of yarn—it significantly outpaces most flyer wheels for high-twist plying of fine yarn.

As shown, this method will cause the spindle to rotate in a counter-clockwise direction. To make it rotate clockwise, you can switch hands or start with the left hand farther back and pushing forward.

Cable-Plying on a Spindle

A cabled yarn, at its most basic, is a yarn that has been plied once in the opposite direction from the initial spin for the singles and then plied again in turn in the original spinning twist direction (the opposite direction from that first plying pass). In other words, you spin it, and then you ply it, and then you ply it again. (It may be necessary to add twist on the first plying pass, as some of that twist will be removed in the cabling pass.)

To make a cabled yarn, wind a double-stranded ball of singles and ply it, adding extra plying twist. Wind the two-ply yarn into a center-pull ball. Holding the yarn from the inside and outside of the center-pull ball together, attach them to the spindle and ply them again in the same direction in which you spun the singles.

You aren't required to spindle-ply your spindle-spun yarns. Some spinners choose to ply all their spindle-spun yarns with a wheel, and that can be a great choice. The down side is giving up the portability of the spindle. But taking a plying project with you is possibly even easier than taking your spinning—a multi-stranded ball is more resilient (and smaller) than most unspun fiber. Don't be afraid to try a variety of plying methods with your spindles. Before you

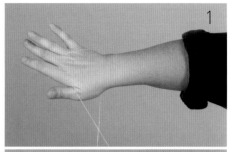

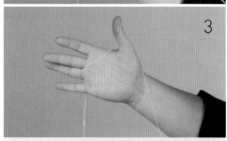

how to **ply andean-style**

1   With the two-stranded ball in your pocket or safely out of the way but accessible, wind the yarn coming out of the ball across the back of the pinkie and ring fingers, then between the ring and middle fingers to the front of the hand. From there, it goes across the palm to the thumb, goes behind the thumb, and then attached to the spindle. You can use either hand, but one hand will be your yarn control hand and the other your spindle hand.

2   Opening and closing the gap between ring and middle fingers provides one layer of flow control for the yarn, as does changing the angle your hand is at as the yarn passes over the back of your thumb. When your hand is more horizontal, yarn will slip through your fingers and past your thumb.

3   When your hand is more vertical, the yarn won't slip through your fingers.

how to **ply andean-style** (continued)

4 Hold the tip of your spindle's shaft in the pocket between the base of your thumb and the palm of your hand. Press your thumb lightly toward your hand to keep it there.

5 Bring your yarn-control hand in toward your body and place the fingertips at the base of the palm of your spindle-holding hand. There will be a loop of yarn dangling between your hands; you need it for your spindle to launch and spin.

6 Push your yarn-control hand forward and out past your spindle-holding hand, releasing the spindle with the thumb that temporarily held it in place.

7 The spindle will fly off your hands, whizzing extremely fast. Let more yarn to be plied slip from your multi-strand ball and pay out a length of yarn across your chest, across your spindle-holding hand, and down to the ground.

8 When the spindle nears the ground, stop letting yarn feed out from your plying ball. Move your spindle-holding hand back and forth along the yarn to help the twist even itself out through the length of yarn you are plying.

9 When you feel there is sufficient plying twist in your yarn, use the butterfly method (see page 86) to walk the spindle up to your spindle-holding hand and grasp it.

10 Keep using the butterfly to store the yarn between your yarn-control hand and your spindle-holding hand.

   Slip off the half-hitch (or half-hitches) and unwind the yarn spiraled up the spindle's shaft. Wind your freshly plied yarn on the cop, spiraling the last bit up the shaft and securing it with one or more half-hitches. (Why more than one? To insure against half-hitch slippage when you're setting the spindle in motion.)

PLYING STRUCTURES

How you choose to structure your plied yarns can have a huge impact on the uses to which the yarn is most suited. Here are some general guidelines, though to be sure of your results, you will need to do samples and swatch them in the intended manner of use.

PLYING STRUCTURE	HOW IT'S MADE	TRAITS
Two-ply	Two singles, both spun in the same direction, plied together in the opposite direction.	Two-ply yarns are commonly used for weaving and lace knitting. They do not have a perfectly smooth surface.
Three-ply	Three singles, all spun in the same direction, plied together in the opposite direction.	Three- (or more than three-) ply yarns have a smoother surface than two-ply yarns and are generally rounder and more popular for knitting non-lace fabrics. When woven, they create very drapey fabrics.
Cabled yarn	Two or more plied yarns that are then plied a second time in the opposite direction of the first plying pass (the same direction in which the original singles were spun).	Cabled yarns have excellent stitch definition and wear well. The cable structure can make even very irregular singles into a consistent yarn. They are very strong and can make even short-stapled or weaker fibers into strong yarn.
Chained singles (also known as Navajo plying)	A singles yarn that is chained (as in crochet) while being twisted in the opposite direction from which it was spun.	Chained singles appears very similar to three-ply, but it isn't as strong. It is commonly used to preserve color repeats.

know it, you might find yourself, as I did in my childhood, taking your plying with you when you go out to play!

Chain-Plying on a Spindle

Chain-plying, sometimes called Navajo plying, is a means of making a cord that looks very similar to a three-ply yarn. Unlike a true three-ply, in which three individual singles are plied together, a chain-plied yarn (also sometimes called a chained singles) has only one singles yarn in it; the effect is achieved by looping the yarn back on itself repeatedly, much like a crochet chain. The resulting yarn does not reap the structural benefits of a true three-ply and is commonly used to preserve color repeats.

Pull out about an armspan's length of yarn and fold back on itself to make a loop. Pinch where the end meets the yarn supply and slip your hand into the loop. Grasp the yarn to be plied and, without letting go of your pinched loop, pull the yarn you just grasped through the loop, forming a new loop.

Secure the end of your looped yarn to your spindle. You can do this by tying it on, attaching it to a hook, or using a leader and joining it with twist.

Pinching twist at the base of your loop so your loop stays open, pull your new loop through for about a foot. The exact distance is up to you, but a foot is reasonably easy to manage.

Reach through and pull up your new loop. Keep your hand inside the loop so it doesn't close up entirely, and set your spindle in motion with the other hand.

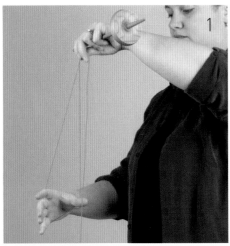

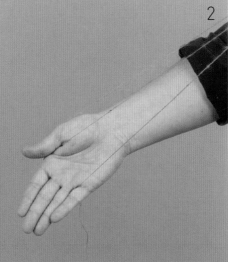

Guide the twist up into your looped yarn, taking care to leave yourself enough space to pull your next loop through.

When you have enough length of yarn to wind on, let your current working loop slide back onto your wrist, and walk your plied yarn up your fingers to keep it under tension so you can wind on. Wind on, then secure your yarn again, and resume plying.

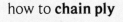

Chain plying preserves the color order of singles.

how to **chain ply**

1 To begin, make a loop, pinch both ends closed, and pull the next length of singles through the loop. Secure the ends to your spindle.

2 Hold the loop open and grasp the next length of singles to be plied, keeping all strands under even tension.

3 Pull the next length of singles through the loop, creating a new loop, and guide the twist into all three strands simultaneously. Continue pulling lengths of yarn through into new loops and guiding the twist into them.

4 When you have plied as much as you can manage in one arm's length, walk the spindle up by winding the yarn onto your hand, then wind the plied yarn onto the spindle.

LIVING WITH SPINDLES

Spindles are durable and low maintenance, but they're not completely foolproof. It is possible for spindles to be damaged or broken or develop quirks that prevent them from performing the way you want. Once you've acquired some spindles you love, you may find yourself asking how best to store them, pack them, and carry them with you, and how to fix them if need be.

Some new spinners worry that children or pets might get hold of spindles and hurt themselves, but fairy tales notwithstanding, that's relatively hard to do. Most spindles are no more dangerous than a sharpened pencil. Some, like metal tahklis, can have very sharp points (such as knitting needles) and are best secured away from inquisitive toddlers. But for the most part, the biggest risks aren't to you or your loved ones but to your spindles or your projects.

Storage

Every spindle is unique, and what works for storing one spindle may not be ideal for another. Your specialty spindles may require specialty storage solutions. Spindles are also beautiful, and you may want to store them in a way that keeps them on display. Here are a few great storage and display ideas, many of them borrowed from fabulous fiber shops with lots of spindles.

Some spindlecrafters and fine woodworkers make specialty racks to hold spindles, and these are also a beautiful and functional way to store your spindles. But many spinners prefer simply to fill their living spaces with them. My own life is like that: there are spindles tucked into bookshelves, in cups on my desk or end table, lying on the kitchen counter with a project in progress. Spindles in use generally hold up well to this approach, but if you have small children, pets, or little space, you may want to find a principled way to store your tools.

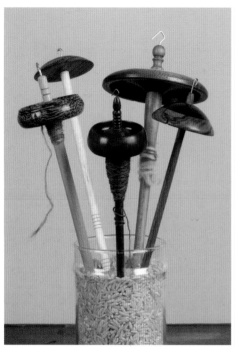

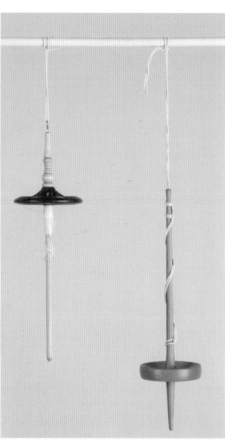

Above: Rice helps hold the spindles upright and absorbs excess moisture. Right: Spindles with and without hooks can be suspended for storage.

Top Whorls

Top-whorl spindles can easily be placed in a cup or vase, but being of different lengths they may be prone to bumping into each other, and it may be hard to fish out just the one you're after when you want to work with it. My favorite solution also solves the problem of varying humidity, which poses a potential risk of warping for some woods (and a problem for spindle shafts): Fill your vase with raw white or brown rice and place the spindle shafts into that.

The rice holds the spindles secure and absorbs any excess moisture in the air, keeping it out of exotic spindle woods. Even in very dry climates, spindles in regular use will get oils from your hands and don't need much maintenance, but you may want to supplement this by rubbing gently with a carnauba or beeswax polish. You don't want to polish spindle shafts perfectly smooth, because if they're too slippery your cop may slip or you may find it unpleasant to spin.

Low Whorls

Low-whorl spindles are a little more complicated. You can store hookless low-whorl spindles by putting them in the rice upside-down, but you may not be looking at the prettiest part of the spindle. If your low whorls have hooks, you may not want to stick the hook into the rice. For spindles with notches, it would be annoying at best to have rice caught in a clever notch, and at worst, you could break the notch trying to get the rice out.

You can store top and bottom whorls by hanging them. While you can just string a line and hang them right from that, they may slip around on the line and slide toward the middle, creating a jumble. One shop I visit has solved this by mounting curtain rods to the wall and hanging loops of string from those at regular intervals, into which the hooks can be placed so the spindles hang neatly. Cup hooks at the edge of a shelf would also work great for this approach.

Hanging by a string means you can also hang spindles that don't have notches or hooks: just attach a leader to your spindle (see page 54) and tie a knot securing the two ends. Spiral the leader up the shaft and use a half-hitch to secure the leader, then hang your spindle from the loop in your leader.

I store support spindles in a drawer or box, nestled in fiber or nice cloth.

Mishaps and Remedies

Ironically, the biggest threat to your spindles is probably damage from dropping them. Dropping spindles on hard surfaces can result in chips, cracks, and bent hooks. Not all chips and cracks are serious enough to keep the spindle from being useful, but it is a risk. If you have very precious spindles, you may not want to choose those for long walks or spinning boundary-pushing yarns.

You may find that a tiny nick or ding in your spindle that you can barely see wants to snag your fiber. With most wooden spindles, you can sand or buff these out easily using fine-grit sandpaper or a fine emery board or nail buffer. If you are in doubt, ask the maker of your spindle.

Many spindles are not glued together, but are fitted carefully with friction holding the whorl to the shaft. A drop can sometimes loosen the whorl without actually damaging anything. Usually, you can slip it right back where it was, but it may not want to stay. A great solution is to wrap a tiny bit of fiber around the spindle's shaft, then slide the whorl onto that, using the fiber as a shim. This often works if you have a loose whorl for any reason, including changes in climate or humidity. If all else fails, wrap a little yarn tightly underneath the whorl (if you're spinning with a top whorl, your cop counts!) and you can keep going; a loose whorl doesn't have to stop you from spinning immediately.

The whorls of these Andean spindles are shimmed. At left, a small piece of wood holds the whorl in place; at right, some fiber does the job.

Safety First

To avoid spindle disasters, I try to follow a few basic rules:

* Never put a spindle on a seat.
* Never put a spindle on the floor.
* Before walking away from a spindle laid on a flat surface, make sure it isn't rolling.
* Don't leave spindles where they'll be attractive to a pet.
* Secure yarn neatly before putting down a spindle and walking away from it.
* Don't leave hooks poking out of an open-topped bag.
* Don't put a spindle bag down on a seat.
* While I wish I could say I was smart enough to just know these things, the sad truth is that each of these rules is one I've made in the wake of an incident that resulted in damage or loss of a spindle or yarn. You will undoubtedly find your own additions to this list, and you will be in good company: that of every spindle spinner for tens of thousands of years.

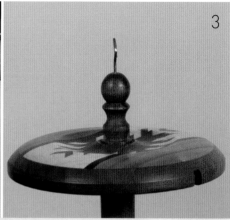

how to **adjust a hook**

1 The hook on this spindle is a bit out of alignment.

2 With pliers that won't mar the wire, tweak the hook very gently into alignment.

3 After a slight adjustment, the hook is centered.

A bent hook, on the other hand, can prevent you from using a spindle happily. There are lots of kinds of hooks, and it can be hard to tell just by looking whether the hook has bent or come out of alignment. To check, you need to hold the spindle suspended from yarn wound on it. See if the yarn is coming out centered over the spindle's axis of rotation. If it isn't, you may get wobbling or erratic spin, and you may find the yarn doesn't want to stay put in the hook.

With most hook damage incurred in a fall from spinning height, your fingers or small pliers can fix it. Before you go to town with the pliers, though, check to make sure the hook isn't loose. If it's loose, you may need to take more drastic action to fix your spindle. Check with the spindle's maker to find out if they have any special tips for you. If the hook is still secure and just a little bent, you should be able to correct this by gently tweaking it with pliers. You may need to adjust forward or back, side to side, or both. When in doubt, ask the maker of your spindle. Changing or fixing a hook should be done with care, and there is no single rule for how (or if) you should attempt this.

Easy Does It

When making a minor spindle repair, remember to be gentle. It's not uncommon to damage a spindle more with an attempted repair than the original ailment. That doesn't mean you shouldn't try it, but if you have any doubts, ask first. There is no better source of advice than your spindle's maker or the shop where you bought it. Many popular spindlecrafters have Internet mailing lists and websites with lots of information both from the makers and fellow spindle owners. These can be a terrific resource. The makers of the finest spindles will often help you out if they're damaged. They want you to use those spindles without fear. If you do crack or chip a spindle, contact the maker and see what they suggest.

SPINDLE REPAIR KIT

I always like to have the following on hand in case one of my spindles needs repair. With this assortment of tools, I can fix almost anything that goes wrong with a spindle, unless it's a catastrophic failure (such as sitting or stepping on a spindle or a severe break in the whorl).

1 **Needle-nose or round-nose pliers** for fixing hooks; round-nose are often better, as needle-nose may mar the metal of your hook

2 **Emery board and fine nail buffer** for minimal smoothing of rough spots

3 **Small rubber bands** to secure things if yarn isn't working to shim a whorl, or to use as a stop for your cop on a slippery shaft

4 **Pocket knife or multitool** for small cutting, poking, and scraping

5 **Matches or a lighter** to warm metal before bending it and check for cracks that are hard to see

6 **Small flashlight** in case I can't have matches or a lighter

7 **Hand cream** to smooth out anything I had to cut or buff, plus my hands need it!

8 **Lip balm** smooths rough spots

9 **Crochet hook** for sampling fibers and the plyback test

10 **Tape measure** for a quick check of TPI or WPI

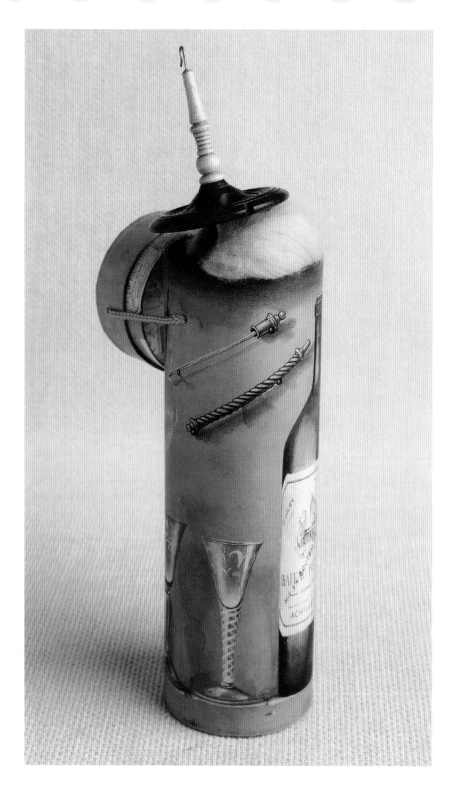

Taking It on the Road

I'll probably always be on the lookout for the perfect spindle bag, and I'll probably always be changing my mind about what it would be like. That's partly because I travel with lots of different kinds of spindles. I usually have at least one rugged, inexpensive, hookless low whorl and one featherweight high whorl with me, along with the selection of repair tools, plus at least one kind of fiber.

Despite all my searching, my favorite spindle bag remains a simple one. I like it because it allows very easy storage and access to my spindle. It's small enough that I resist the temptation to carry dozens of spindles and pounds of fiber, plus it doesn't get in the way while I'm walking around spinning. I leave it always packed with a project (or maybe two) and ready to grab when I'm walking out the door.

One problem with this approach is that the fiber in my spindle bag tends to get roughed up. A more organized spinner might prevent this by finding hard-sided storage that fits in a spindle bag. I usually just put my fiber in a plastic bag inside the spindle bag, leaving it open so I can readily pull out a tuft of it to spin while I'm on the go. If the fiber has grown very compacted, I sometimes pull out a larger chunk and carefully attenuate it into a rope I can wrap around my wrist.

I don't generally choose my very finest, most fragile fibers for spinning out and about. If they're too fussy and delicate, they're prone to damage in a spindle bag, and they present too great a risk of yarn breaking and dropping a spindle. Walking around is a great time to do a lot of plying, because there's usually plenty of space for large, expansive movements (see page 107) and a securely wound ball will do very well in a spindle bag.

Opposite: Hard-sided gift boxes for wine make great spindle storage. Above: A tall wide-mouthed water bottle can be just the right size for a small spindle and some fiber. Right: This specially designed carrying case protects my spindle in style.

Have Spindle, Will Travel

Packing for a longer trip, where spindles will go in a suitcase, I like to pad them with fiber and put them inside something hard-sided. Some great solutions are wide-mouthed water bottles, the sturdy tubes used to pack bottled beverages for shipping, or the can tennis balls come in. These can hold a spindle and lots of fiber and prevent annoyances like having a hook get caught on clothing inside your luggage.

I almost always have inexpensive spindles with me that I'd be willing to give away, plus a little bit of fiber suited for teaching a brand-new spinner. I started when I ran into people I'd never see again (like in an airport) who really wanted to learn to spin, and I wished I had something to give them to teach them with. Even on trips where I haven't encountered a teachable moment, I've usually been glad to have the extra spindles. Once in a while, I've needed one myself. There's little more frustrating than being caught out on the road with a project in progress, lots of great fiber for it, and a broken or lost spindle.

If I'm spinning in very close quarters, like on an airplane, a featherweight top whorl is hard to beat. I can use it to spin extremely fine yarn with ease and get a lot of spinning enjoyment out of a small amount of fiber—also great if I'm traveling! The smaller that spindle is, the easier it is to pack it, take out in transit, and put away again. I won't have a lot of elbowroom, so I'll be spinning short lengths of yarn. I won't have as much exposure to outside forces as I would spinning long lengths between wind-ons and waving my spindle around me as I walk. And if I'm sitting at home on the sofa? Well, that's a perfect time to break out a supported spindle.

Spindle-spun Projects

Finding uses for your handspun yarn is one of the great thrills of spinning, and perhaps that's most true for your very earliest efforts—the yarns you spun when you were first getting a feel for the magic that is making yarn out of mere fluff. Your first yarn may not have a lot of yardage, but there are still lots of great uses for even small bits.

ALPACA SILK SHAWL

finished size

62" (157.5 cm) wide along top edge and 22" (56 cm) long from top to point, including edging.

yarn

About 450 yd (411 m) alpaca/tussah blend 2-ply, laceweight.

needles

U.S. size 4 (3.5 mm). Adjust needle size if necessary to obtain the correct gauge.

notions

Split-ring stitch marker (m); tapestry needle.

gauge

Each diamond measures about 5" (12.5 cm) from top to bottom and side to side.

note

The lace edging is attached to the edge of the shawl while knitting. To attach edging, knit the last st of every RS row tog with edge st as foll: insert RH needle into last st of edging row, and with RS of shawl facing insert RH needle through st or row at edge as if to pick up and knit st, then draw loop through edge and last edging st to knit tog. On WS rows, slip the first st with yarn in front (as indicated in the chart). Make sure to work through every CO loop along CO edges and every other row along garter edges.

To turn corner at lower edge of shawl, work one repeat of Lace Edging pattern, working last st of every RS row into same st at lower point of shawl.

Spun with low twist, alpaca produces a drapey fabric but is prone to stretching. When spun firmly, alpaca can lose the soft hand, but it wears wonderfully. Silk is lightweight, has great tensile strength, and can withstand a great deal of twist. Adding silk to alpaca lightens the yarn and keeps the high-twist yarn from stiffening, making the blended yarn stronger than the two fibers spun separately. The modular construction of this shawl makes it perfect for color-changing yarns.

Diamond and Triangle Layout

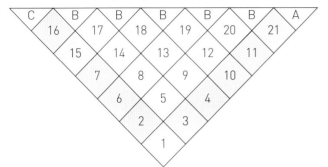

- ☐ work following instructions for Edge Diamond A
- ☐ work following instructions for Edge Diamond B
- ☐ work following instructions for Inner Diamond

Shawl

First diamond

CO 44 sts. Place marker (pm) after 22 sts.

Row 1 and all odd-numbered rows: (WS) Purl.

Row 2: K3, [yo, ssk] to 3 sts before m, k1, ssk, sl m, k2tog, k1, [k2tog, yo] to last 3 sts, k3—2 sts dec'd.

Row 4: K3, [yo, ssk] to 2 sts before m, ssk, sl m, k2tog, [k2tog, yo] to last 3 sts, k3—2 sts dec'd.

Rep Rows 2–5 until 12 sts rem, ending after a WS row.

Next row: K3, yo, ssk, sl m, k2tog, yo, k3—10 sts rem.

Next row: Purl.

Next row: K3, ssk, sl m, k2tog, k3—8 sts rem.

Next row: Purl.

Next row: K2, ssk, sl m, k2tog, k2—6 sts rem.

Next row: Purl.

Next row: K1, ssk, sl m, k2tog, k1—4 sts rem.

Next row: Purl.

Next row: Ssk, sl m, k2tog—2 sts rem. BO rem sts.

Edge Diamonds

Edge Diamond A: Using knitted method, CO 22 sts, pm, pick up and knit 22 sts along one edge of previous diamond (as shown in diagram). Work as for first diamond.

Edge Diamond B: Pick up and knit 22 sts along one edge of previous diamond (as shown in diagram), pm, using knitted method, CO 22 sts. Work as for first diamond.

Follow Edge Diamond A directions for Diamonds 2, 4, 7, 11, and 16

Follow Edge Diamond B directions for Diamonds 3, 6, 10, 15, and 21.

Inner Diamond

Pick up and knit 22 sts along edge of previous diamond, pm, pick up and knit 22 sts along adjacent diamond (as shown in diagram). Work as for first diamond.

Follow Inner Diamond directions for Diamonds 5, 8, 9, 12–14, and 17–20. If desired, add more rows of diamonds for the desired size.

Lace Edging

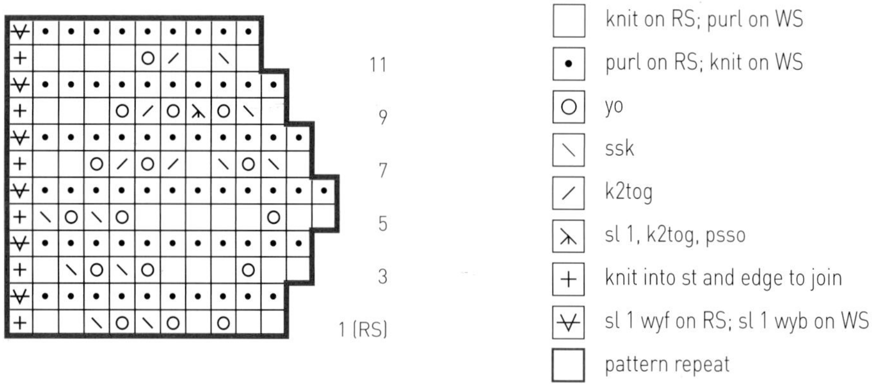

Lace Edging chart with rows numbered 11, 9, 7, 5, 3, 1 (RS)

Legend:
- ☐ knit on RS; purl on WS
- • purl on RS; knit on WS
- ○ yo
- \ ssk
- / k2tog
- ⅄ sl 1, k2tog, psso
- + knit into st and edge to join
- V sl 1 wyf on RS; sl 1 wyb on WS
- ☐ pattern repeat

Top Triangles

Triangle A: Using knitted method, CO 22 sts, pick up and knit 22 sts along edge of Diamond 21, pm. Work as for First Diamond until 22 sts rem. Sl rem sts to holder or scrap yarn.

Triangle B: Pick up and knit 22 sts along each of two adjacent diamonds (as for Inner Diamond), pm. Work as for First Diamond until 22 sts rem. Sl rem sts to holder or scrap yarn. Repeat for remaining 4 spaces between 2 diamonds along top edge.

Triangle C: Pick up and knit 22 sts along edge of Diamond 16, pm, using knitted method, CO 22 sts. Work as for First Diamond until 22 sts rem. Sl rem sts to holder or scrap yarn.

Finishing
Crochet edging

With crochet hook, attach yarn to first st at top right edge of shawl. Ch 2, [sc 1 in next st, ch 1] to end, sc in last st. Cut yarn and draw tail through last st to fasten off.

Lace edging

CO 10 sts.
Row 1: (RS) K2, yo, k1, [yo, ssk] twice, k2, k tog last st and edge of shawl—11 sts.
Row 2 and all odd-numbered rows: (WS) Sl 1 wyf, knit to end.
Row 3: K2, yo, k3, [yo, ssk] twice, k1, k tog last st and edge of shawl—12 sts.
Row 5: K2, yo, k5, [yo, ssk] twice, k tog last st and edge of shawl—13 sts.

Row 7: K1, ssk, yo, ssk, k1, [k2tog, yo] twice, k2, k tog last st and edge of shawl—12 sts.
Row 9: K1, ssk, yo, sl 1, k2tog, psso, yo, k2tog, yo, k3, k tog last st and edge of shawl—11 sts.
Row 11: K1, ssk, k1, k2tog, yo, k4, knit tog last st and edge of shawl—10 sts.
Rep Rows 1–12 for the pattern from top left corner to the point (see note above) and back up to the top right corner, ending with Row 12.

Bind off loosely. Use tapestry needle to weave in ends. Block.

your inner PINK

BY DENNY MCMILLAN

finished measurements

Custom; piece shown measures 4½" (11.5 cm) tall and 18½" (47 cm) outer diameter, to fit over a 22" (56 cm) head.

yarn

Tan yarn (outer portion)—Merino/silk/cashmere/yak/camel blended batts, 3-ply worsted weight. Pink yarn (inside lining)—Hand-dyed Merino/silk top, chain-plied worsted weight. Accent yarn—1 ply angora and 1 ply Merino, 2-ply laceweight.

needles

U.S. size 8 (5 mm): two 16" (40 cm) circulars (cir). Adjust needle size if necessary to obtain the right gauge or desired fabric.

notions

Crochet hook; stitch marker; tapestry needle.

gauge

14 sts and 20 rnds = 4" (10 cm) in tan yarn. 14 sts and 26 rnds = 4" (10 cm) in pink yarn.

Knitted from her very first spindle-spun yarns, Denny McMillan's neck-warmer is one of my favorite projects. The soft outer layer is spun from a blend including warm down fibers, and the bold pink lining is a secret spark of color. The fit is completely customizable, so this can be knitted with almost any quantity of yarn—even a short length of something special (here, an angora/Merino two-ply) can make a big impact.

Neck Warmer
Pink lining

Using a provisional method and pink yarn, CO 65 sts. Place marker (pm) and join for working in the rnd, being careful not to twist sts. Work in stockinette stitch (St st) for about 1" (2.5 cm).

Turning rnds

Next rnd: With accent yarn and leaving a long tail, knit, wrapping the needle twice for every st.

Next rnd: Knit, dropping extra wraps as you come to them.

Tan outer layer

With tan yarn, work in St st until piece measures 4½" (11.5 cm) or desired length from turning rnds. Repeat turning rnds.

Pink lining

With pink yarn, work in St st until the lining (including the portion worked at the beginning) is the same length as the outer layer. Remove the provisional CO and place the live sts on the second cir needle. With pink yarn threaded on a tapestry needle, work Kitchener st to graft sts.

Crochet chain edging

With crochet hook and starting at the last double-length st (where extra wraps were dropped) of the first turning rnd, draw up the right half of the knitted st, *draw up the right half of the next st to the right and pull through the first st on the hook to fasten it off; rep from * until 1 st rem. With tail of accent yarn threaded on a tapestry needle, [pass through the rem st, then through the first chain st] 2 times.

Repeat for other turning rnd. Weave in ends.

Variations

* Instead of a provisional CO and Kitchener st, use a loose CO and BO, then join the CO and BO edges with whipstitch or invisible horizontal seam.
* To customize the size and gauge of the piece, work a gauge swatch to find the desired fabric and find the average gauge in stitches per inch. Multiply the head circumference of the recipient by the number of stitches per inch to find the total number of stitches to cast on.

simple crochet hat

finished measurements

20½" (52 cm), to fit an adult head.

yarn

Worsted weight. Merino/silk 2-ply (blue-gray): 98 yd (90 m). Merino 3-ply (white): 30 yd (27 m).

hook

U.S. size H/8 (5 mm). Adjust hook size if necessary to obtain the desired gauge or fabric.

gauge

19 sts and 16 rnds = 4" (10 cm) in fpdc "rib."

stitch guide

Front post double crochet (fpdc): Yarn over, insert hook from front to back to front around the post of the corresponding stitch below, yarn over and pull up a loop [yarn over, draw through two loops on hook] twice.

Crocheted in the round from one skein of merino/silk two-ply and one skein of merino three-ply, this is a great project for your first few skeins. Use as many first skeins as you like, swapping them out to make stripes. The major benefit to making a hat this way is that you can try it on many times as you go to make sure it fits.

Hat

Rnd 1: With gray, Ch 4; join with sl st to form ring.

Rnd 2: Ch2, hdc 11 in ring—12 sts.

Rnd 3: Ch 2, [sc 2 in same st] across rnd, sl st in beg ch 2 to join—25 sts.

Rnd 4: Ch 2, hdc 2, [hdc 2 in same st, hdc 3] 5 times, hdc 2 in same st, hdc 2, sl st in beg ch2 to join—32 sts.

Rnd 5: Ch 2, hdc 32, sl st in beg ch 2 to join—33 sts.

Rnd 6: Ch 2, hdc, [hdc 2 in same st, hdc 2] 10 times, hdc 2 in same st, sl st in beg ch2 to join—44 sts.

Rnd 7: Ch 2, [hdc 2 in same st, hdc 1] 21 times, sl st in beg ch2 to join—64 sts.

Rnd 8: Ch 2, hdc in each st around, sl st in beg ch2 to join.

Rnd 9: Ch 2, *fpdc, sc; rep from * to last hdc, end with fpdc, sl st in beg ch2 to join.

Rnd 10: Ch 2, *fpdc, sc 2 in same st; rep from * around, sl st in beg ch2 to join—96 sts.

Rnd 11: Ch 2, *fpdc, sc in same st, fpdc, sc; rep from * around, sl st in beg ch2 to join—128 sts.

Rnd 12: Ch2, * fpdc, sc; rep from * around, sl st in beg ch2 to join.

Rnds 13 and 14: Rep Rnd 12.

Rnd 15: (dec rnd) Ch 2, *fpdc, sc 2; rep from * around, sl st in beg ch2 to join—96 sts.

Rnd 16: Ch2, *fpdc, sc; rep from * around, sl st in beg ch2 to join—64 sts.

Rnd 17: Ch 2, *fpdc, sc 2; rep from * around, sl st in beg ch2 to join—96 sts.

Rnds 18–20: Rep Rnd 17.

Rnd 21: With white, work 1 rnd even.

Rnds 22–25: Rep Rnd 15—64 sts rem.

Fasten off. Weave in ends.

cotton washcloth

Cotton is a tremendously absorbent fiber, making it an excellent choice for fabrics for kitchen and bath. Our gentle washcloth is spun from organic cotton. The singles were spun using a support spindle, then wound together into a four-stranded ball from which they were plied very firmly. This makes for strong and consistent yarn even if there are slubs in the singles—which may add absorbency and texture.

finished size

About 5½" (14 cm) square.

yarn

About 40 yd (37 m) organic cotton 4-ply, fingering weight. Thanks to Sarah Swett for the cotton yarn shown here.

needles

U.S. size 4 (3.5 mm). Adjust needle size if necessary to obtain the desired gauge or fabric.

notions

Stitch markers (optional); tapestry needle.

gauge

23 sts and 48 rows = 4" (10 cm) in patt.

note

For Rows 8–90, work RS rows following chart and knit WS rows. As there is no patterning on WS rows, only RS rows are shown.

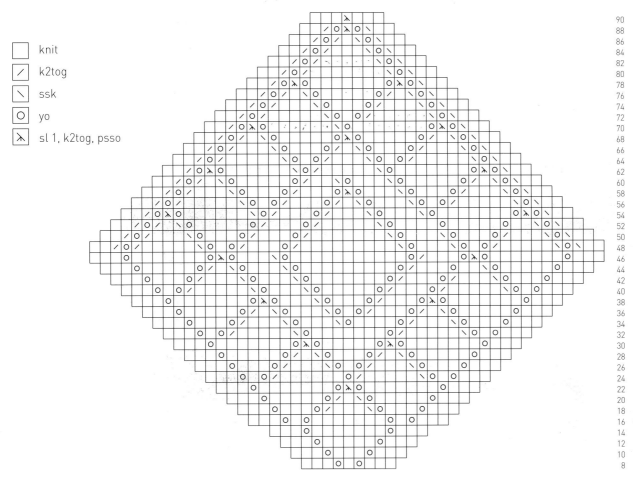

▢	knit
╱	k2tog
╲	ssk
○	yo
⋏	sl 1, k2tog, psso

Row numbers (right side of chart, bottom to top): 8, 10, 12, 14, 16, 18, 20, 22, 24, 26, 28, 30, 32, 34, 36, 38, 40, 42, 44, 46, 48, 50, 52, 54, 56, 58, 60, 62, 64, 66, 68, 70, 72, 74, 76, 78, 80, 82, 84, 86, 88, 90

Washcloth

CO 1 st.

Row 1: K1f&b—2 sts.

Row 2: K1, k1f&b—3 sts.

Row 3: K1, k1f&b, k1—4 sts.

Row 4: K1, k1f&b, k2—5 sts.

Row 5: K2, k1f&b, k2—6 sts.

Row 6: K2, k1f&b, k3—7 sts.

Row 7 and all WS rows to Row 89: Knit.

Row 8 and all RS rows to Row 90: Work
  Washcloth chart.

Row 91: K1, k2tog, knit to end—1 st
  dec'd.

Rep Row 91 four more times—2 sts rem.

Row 96: K2tog. Cut yarn and draw tail
  through rem st. Weave in ends.

resources

The publisher gratefully acknowledges the following for providing materials and tools used in this book: Louet North America; Sarah Swett; Schacht Spindle Company; Shuttles, Spindles, and Skeins; The Spinning Loft; and Spunky Eclectic.

Spindles & Tools

Alden Amos
pweb.jps.net/~gaustad
Cover, pages 38, 92

Jonathan and Sheila Bosworth
journeywheel.com
Cover, pages 18, 31, 46, 67, 78, 83, 87, 88, 119

Cascade Spindle Company
cascadespindles.com
Pages 12, 22

Center for Traditional Textiles of Cusco
textilescusco.org
Pages 17, 25, 100, 109, 114

Collection of Ann Budd
Page 40

Collection of Linda Ligon
Pages 18, 21, 24, 79

Collection of Maggie Casey
Page 31

Tom Forrester
Woodshaper Studios
Cover, pages 27, 29, 30, 81, 99, 105, 114, 118

Golding Fiber Tools
goldingfibertools.com
Pages 4, 21, 103

Grafton Fibers
graftonfibers.com
Pages 66, 119

Greensleeves Spindles
greensleevesspindles.com
Pages 10, 17, 26, 31, 32, 45, 102, 105, 114

Anne Grout
Cover, pages 17, 88, 90

Hatchtown Farm
hatchtown.com
Cover, pages 12, 20, 27, 55, 75, 88, 116

Jenkins Woodworking
jenkinswoodworking.com
Pages 88, 97–98

Kundert Spindles
kundertspindles.com
Pages 14, 17, 59–60, 114, 116

Lily Spindles
lilyspindles.com
Page 18

Louet North America
louet.com
Pages 17, 20, 107

Magpie Woodworks
magpiewoodworksusa.com
Cover, pages 10, 12, 15, 17, 35, 42, 44, 48, 75, 84, 88, 89, 111, 114

Schacht Spindle Co.
schachtspindleco.com
Pages 18, 20, 34, 36, 39, 50, 54, 57–58, 61, 71, 82, 96, 103

Thomas L. Sheridan
heritagespinning.com
Page 15

Spindlewood Co.
spindlewoodco.com
Pages 2, 21, 68, 75, 102, 103, 114

Edward Tabachek
mts.net/~tabachek/
Pages 10, 12, 18, 56, 63, 94, 102, 114

Trindle Spindles
trindleman.etsy.com
Page 28

Woodchuck
Rod "Woody" Stevens (retired)
Pages 15, 29, 104, 114

Fiber

Abby's Yarns
abbysyarns.com

Louet North America
louet.com

Spunky Eclectic
spunkyeclectic.com

BIBLIOGRAPHY

Amos, Alden. *The Alden Amos Big Book of Handspinning*. Loveland, Colorado: Interweave, 2001.

Brown, Rachel. *The Weaving, Spinning, and Dyeing Book*. New York: Knopf, 1983.

Casey, Maggie. *Start Spinning: Everything You Need to Know to Make Great Yarn*. Loveland, Colorado: Interweave, 2008.

Claydon, Jennifer. *Spin, Dye, Stitch: How to Create and Use Your Own Yarns*. Cincinnati, Ohio: North Light Books, 2009.

Delaney, Connie. *Spindle Spinning from Novice to Expert*. Corinth, Kentucky: Kokovoko Press, 1998.

Field, Anne. *The Ashford Book of Spinning*. Canterbury, New Zealand: Shoal Bay Press, 1999.

Fournier, Nola, and Jane Fournier. *In Sheep's Clothing: A Handspinner's Guide to Wool*. Loveland, Colorado: Interweave, 1995.

Garripoli, Amelia. *Productive Spindling*. Port Angeles, Washington: The Bellwether, 2009.

Gibson-Roberts, Priscilla. *Spinning in the Old Way: How (and Why) to Make Your Own Yarn with a High-Whorl Handspindle*. Fort Collins, Colorado: Nomad Press, 2006. (Previously published as *High Whorling: A Spinner's Guide to an Old-world Skill*.)

Hochberg, Bette. *Handspindles*. Santa Cruz, California: B. and B. Hochberg, 1977.

———. *Spin Span Spun: Facts and Folklore for Spinners and Weavers*. Santa Cruz, California: B. and B. Hochberg, 1979.

Irwin, Bobbie. *The Spinner's Companion*. Loveland, Colorado: Interweave, 2001.

Jenkins, David. *The Cambridge History of Western Textiles*. Cambridge and New York: Cambridge University Press, 2003.

King, Amy. *Spin Control: Techniques for Spinning the Yarns You Want*. Loveland, Colorado: Interweave, 2009.

Kroll, Carol. *The Whole Craft of Spinning: From the Raw Material to the Finished Yarn*. New York: Dover Publications, 1981.

Ligon, Linda Collier. *This Is How I Go When I Go Like This: Weaving and Spinning as Metaphor*. Loveland, Colorado: Interweave, 2004.

Linder, Olive and Harry Linder. *Handspinning Cotton*. Phoenix, Arizona: The Cotton Squares, 1977.

MacKenzie McCuin, Judith. *The Intentional Spinner: A Holistic Approach to Making Yarn*. Loveland, Colorado: Interweave, 2008.

Raven, Lee. *Hands On Spinning*. Loveland, Colorado: Interweave, 1987.

———. *Spin It: Making Yarn from Scratch*. Loveland, CO: Interweave, 2003.

Simmons, Paula. *Spinning for Softness and Speed*. Seattle, Washington: Madrona, 1982.

Spin-Off Magazine. A Handspindle Treasury: 20 Years of Spinning Wisdom from Spin-Off *Magazine*. Loveland, Colorado: Interweave, 2000.

Stove, Margaret. *Handspinning, Dyeing, and Working with Merino and Superfine Wools*. Loveland, Colorado: Interweave, 1991.

index